# THE

# *STANZAS OF DZJN*

# *THEOGENESIS*

## *(1915)*

Contents: Stanzas of Dzjn; Foundation of
Hermetic Philosophy; Hermetic, Atlantean,
Mayan, Akkadian, Chaldean, Egyptian & Persian
Brotherhoods.

DE

MERCURIUS    MERCURIO

# *Dr. A.S. Raleigh*

ISBN 0-7661-0055-3

# THE
# STANZAS OF DZJN
# THEOGENESIS

With Commentary by

## DR. A. S. RALEIGH

(Hach-mactzin) Master Elder Brother, H. B. of A.

HERMETIC PUBLISHING COMPANY
SAN DIEGO, CALIF.
PRICE $2.50

# CONTENTS.

## PART TWO.

### THE FOUNDATION OF HERMETIC PHILOSOPHY.

# PREFACE.

The "Stanzas of Dzjn" is a book of poetry, dealing with the history of Creative Evolution from the earliest dawn of Creative Action down to the final consummation, when the Universe returns into the Bosom of Infinity. There are reasons for believing that in its original Form, it was the product of the Nagas of Ancient India, though as we have it now, it is undoubtedly influenced greatly by Hindoo and Thibetan elements. These Stanzas have for a number of centuries been in the custody of the Buddhist Monasteries of Lahdak. It was there that Madame Blavatsky obtained a number of the Stanzas. Some of these she published together with her Commentaries, under the Title of The Secret Doctrine as Anthropogenesis, and Cosmogenesis. These Stanzas and Commentaries will be found in the First and Second Volumes of the Secret Doctrine.

It was her intention to later on publish certain of the Stanzas following these, but her untimely death prevented this. The later Stanzas dealing with Theogenesis, or the Evolution of the Divine Nature in Man, remained unpublished for a number of years. In the course of time, they fell into the hands of The Temple of the People, who published them in the Temple Artisan. In this way they fell into the hands of the Author, who was requested to write a Commentary on them. This he did, the Temple of the People promising to publish it. He has now waited two years, and they have made not the slightest move in that direction, and hence it becomes evident that if the public are ever to have the benefit of these Commentaries, he must publish them himself. Through the Hermetic Publishing Company, he is now able to bring them out. He has determined to add to them certain articles dealing with Hermetic Philosophy, in order that the reader may the better understand the principles enunciated in the Commentary, these Articles will be found in the Second Part of the book.

The Author trusts that this volume will enable the reader to better understand the Esoteric Kosmogany of the Ancients. He begs to assure the reader that this work is authoritative, and is the last word in such matters, as he has full authority to speak in regard to all Hermetic Mysteries. His reason for publishing these matters at this time is the fact that he is convinced that we are now living in the time of the Great Transition, and that those things which have been kept secret for ages must now be revealed.

He acknowledges his indebtedness to the Temple Artisan for the Text of the Stanzas, from which publication it was taken.

In offering to the public a work on Transcendental Occultism, particularly one dealing with the subject from a purely Kosmical standpoint, the Author realizes that he has much opposition to overcome, on account of the Individualistic view that has grown up in this country, but at the same time, he feels that the interest of Truth and Progress demands that he shall take this stand, and in this spirit, he hands to the people this work on Creative Evolution, viewed from the Esoteric and Hermetic standpoint, feeling that it is the greatest contribution to Hermetic Literature thus far given to the world.

DR. A. S. RALEIGH,

Master Elder Brother,
Hermetic Brotherhood of Atlantis.

Oceano, Calif., Dec. 1st, 1914.

## THE STANZAS OF DZJN

There has been some criticism recently as to the authenticity of the Stanzas of Dzjn, which, together with the Commentaries, have been run in serial form in the columns of Temple Talks. It has been alleged by some of our readers and others who are not our readers that they are not authentic, but are in fact Astral Rubbish. This accusation has been brought against them by the editor of the Word, and by at least two other persons who are looked upon by many as authorities on occult matters. Some of these criticisms are based upon a lack of confidence in the Temple of the People, who first brought these Stanzas to the notice of the public, while others evidently do not like some of the things stated in the Stanzas. Now it is evident that in literary criticism we must confine our criticism to the merits of the particular piece of literature, and not be influenced by our opinion of those who have given it circulation. The real question for each one of us to solve is this: Do the Stanzas upon their face indicate that they are authentic? The question of authenticity is in reality a question of whether they are a bona fide continuation of the Stanzas commented upon in the Secret Doctrine, or forgeries that are designed to pass for such continuation.

In criticism of this nature there are but two elements that may enter into the equation, viz., style and the nature of the Doctrines taught. The style of the Stanzas of Theogenesis and that of the Stanzas of Kosmogenesis and Anthropogenesis is identical. This demonstrates that they were all written by the same party, or else that the Stanzas of Theogenesis were forged by some one able to exactly duplicate the style of the original Stanzas. When one realizes the great difficulty which anyone meets with in an effort to duplicate the style of another this seems impossible. Then we must bear in mind that in this case the difficulty is greatly increased by reason of the fact that there are in both sections of the Stanzas numerous technical terms belonging to a Dead Language with which not one connected with the Temple of the People is at all familiar, and also that there are technical terms connected with religious ideas as well as philosophical doctrines of which the leaders of the Temple of the People are entirely ignorant. Add to this the fact that these Stanzas are in the form of Oriental Poetry, and that the meter had to be preserved as well as all the other matters, the difficulty in the way of a forgery that would not be transparent at first glance becomes well nigh unsurmountable.

Now, when we come to the other element of criticism, viz., that of Doctrine, the difficulty in the way of forgery becomes even greater. It is to be borne in mind that the Stanzas of Dzjn are in reality a work on Creative Evolution. The Stanzas of Kosmogenesis deal with the Evolutionary Forces that were operative in the engendering of the Kosmos. Throughout this entire series there is presented a certain theory of Evolution. In the Stanzas of Anthropogenesis this same Theory of Evolution is applied to the generation of Man, showing that it is the same system that is operative throughout the two sections of the Stanzas. Now, in the Stanzas of Theogenesis we find the workings of the Creative Evolutionary Process applied to the Evolution of Godhood in Man. It is evident that Theogenesis gives to us the workings of the identical forces that have in the past evolved the Kosmos and Man. Not only is this true, but it is the same Theory of Evolution that is brought out in these later Stanzas. The Stanzas of Theogenesis give us exactly what we would expect to find as a result of what was given in the previous Stanzas, provided we understood the Theory taught in the former Stanzas. That is to say, Theogenesis is the logical outgrowth of Anthropogenesis. Now it may be alleged that Mrs. La Due and Dr. Dower were familiar with the Principles involved, and that they formulated a system of Stanzas that would give expression to the same Principles. This would apply if they knew the inner meaning of the former Stanzas and had the Logical capacity to work out the future Evolution of Man, neither of which propositions is true of them.

There is another matter that must be taken into consideration at this stage of our inquiry. There has at all times been an Esoteric Science of Evolution, which has been fully understood by certain men. This Science not only covers the Evolution of the past, but, dealing in Universal Principles, covers that which is to be. There are those who perfectly understand this Evolutionary Process and what the work of Theogenesis will be. Now the Stanzas of Theogenesis in their entirety, so far as their Inner Meaning is concerned, are an exact duplicate of that Esoteric Tradition as to the Future work of Creative Evolution. Is this a coincidence? Or was the Author of them familiar with the Esoteric Science of Creative Evolution and was he writing in the form of Poetry that which we know to be the true Science of Theogenesis? This Esoteric Key is not known to either B. S., R. S. or to the Author of the Commentary signed by the Symbol of Hilarian, whoever he might be. We know this, for their Commentaries manifest the grossest ignorance of the Esoteric Meaning of the Stanzas, and therefore we know that neither one of them is in possession of the Esoteric Tradition. Is it at all likely that one ignorant of the Esoteric Science could write something in which the Esoteric Science was perfectly revealed and never make a single mistake?

However, this is not all that we have to consider. The Esoteric Science makes use of a definite system of Symbolism, therefore the Tradition can either be written in philosophic terms or else in the form of the Sacred Symbolism. Were an Epopt to undertake to write a work on Theogenesis in the language of Sacred Symbolism he would use every one of the Symbols used in our Stanzas in exactly the same sense as they are there used. We know that the persons who are accused of forging these Stanzas did not know the Sacred Symbols, for in their Commentaries they have manifested the most erroneous views concerning them, notwithstanding the fact that they had previously had access to a Commentary giving their correct meaning. When people are so ignorant of the meaning of the Sacred Symbols that they cannot recognize the true interpretation when they see it, is it at all reasonable to suppose that they will be able to make use of them in their exact sense while making a forgery? Given a person ignorant of the Esoteric Tradition and likewise of the Sacred Symbols, is it at all probable that he will stumble onto a method by which he can write the Esoteric Tradition in the form of its proper Symbols? Will Mrs. La Due's bitterest enemies assert that she is a master of the Mystery of the Sacred Animals? Yet those Sacred Animals are made use of in the Stanzas of Theogenesis in the sense in which none but a Beholder could use them. If those Stanzas were originally written in the Temple, they were written by an Epopt, and I do not presume that the most militant member of the Temple would assert that there are any Epoptae at Halcyon! Furthermore, there are matters taught in the Stanzas that the Temple does not accept. In the Commentary now running in Temple Talks it is conclusively proven that, according to the Stanzas, we are now in the Sixth Round, and that the 10th Avatar is now living upon the Earth, and this is flatly contrary to the Teaching of the Temple. Is it at all likely that they would consciously put out something that contradicted their own teaching? If they understood the Inner Meaning of the Stanzas they would teach altogether different to what they do. Is it thinkable that a people would forge something that they themselves did not understand? Forgeries are not made in that way. For the reasons above indicated, and for others which we have no space to enumerate, it is evident that the Stanzas are an authentic fragment of the Esoteric Tradition, and that therefore the Temple of the People has merely passed it on to others.

## THE STANZAS OF DZJN.

## THEOGENESIS.

### (Text: Temple Artisan, 1906, 1912, 1913.)

### Stanza I.

1. Since Fohat gathered two lines of fire in a close embrace, forming a circle of flame to make room for the feet of the Fifth, have the demi-Gods been filling that Kosmic field with images of themselves.

2. To and fro have the first-born run, darting behind each Flaming Sword that sprang from the head of the Mighty One, while seeking for Pasture against the day of the birth of the great Red Cow. The milk of that cow will gather and flow in rivers of Water and Wine to quench the thirst of the twice-born Lords of the Sacred Mystic Fire.

### Stanza II.

3. Said the Radiant One to the Shining Face: I will cause a shade to cover thee for a day and a night of time. I will brood thy young, and bring them forth in strength and might when the shade has passed from thy face and thou shinest forth once more.

4. For thou shalt shine again with seven-fold light, and the face of thy First-born Son shall reflect the light that shines from thine own. The black and brown shall be no more, and the golden-hued shall awaken from sleep, and rule as they ruled of yore.

5. Fire and flood, acid and blood, shall flow in streams and drench the star with the blackened face. The once bright sons of the demi-Gods have cast deep shadows upon that face; they have stolen the fire that lightened its eyes and molded it into a gleaming mass to fetter and bind their once lithe limbs. Vengeance swift will overtake and cast them into the pit.

6. When the circle of flame shall open again and the line of life be loosed from thrall, the five will fall into the six, and Surabhi's teats will deliver four doves —each bearing a branch of the Sacred Ash for the help

and healing of Maya's sons. Fohat will once more cross the line with another and mightier stride, and will draw the downward arc of the line of life to an upward sweep, by the strength of his own right arm.

### Stanzas III.

7. The four-fold Lahs will emit from their loins the germs that shall grow into three-fold coverings of animal forms, of fish and of fowl for the service of man.

8. No more shall huge creatures and crawling things find room on the Rim of the Wheel where dwelleth the Sons of Fire and Flame. The beasts of the field and birds of the air will meet and part in peace, and both shall feed on the purple grain, the gift direct of the Gods. All growths of the under crust of the Wheel shall be thenceforth forbidden, and man shall live by the power of his Will in place of coarser foods. When the Wheel has whirled one crore and a half, the Sparks will embody themselves in a fruit, the like of which no man hath known. The infant as well as the full-grown man shall eat of that fruit, and words of wisdom will fall from its lips, to the wonderment of the Gods.

### Stanza IV.

1. Fohat has lifted his foot, but halts ere he reaches the limit of his stride. The Sons of Flame have cried to him in sore distress: "The Sons of Maya cannot reach the ring, pass not, if thou shalt place thy heavy foot upon their necks before they reach the Chaya of that ring."

2. Fohat lifts his voice, that voice long stilled, and bids the fiery servants of his will to take his ultimatum to the Sons of Flame: "I will not halt for Gods or men, but this much will I do," Go thou to Maya's sons and strike the sacred chord upon the seven stringed lyre within each one. Perchance it may arouse them from their sleep and give them speed to reach the goal ere falls my foot upon the nether side of the dark stream.

3. Back came the messengers and said, "We cannot wake the sacred chord. But five of the seven strings of the lyre will sound, two lie jangling and untuned."

4. Fohat roused to anger, shot forth a stream of fire which circled all the Heavens and awoke the Asuras on the heights. Swiftly on the wind of their own wings came they from the realms of rest and gave speech to Fohat, saying, "Put down thy foot if so thou wilt and close thy stride, but ere thou doest so, know this, ere thou raisest it again we with our brothers, the divine builders, will have given of ourselves to Maya's sons that which thou wouldst now withhold, and the two strings of the lyre will no longer jangle out of tune.

5. When the first full chord is struck then thou shalt die—for thou are old and thy work well nigh done, so cease thine anger and give some space for effort if thou wouldst prolong thine own labors.

### Stanza V.

1. And wilt thou then make bold to cross my will? cried Fohat in his rage. Wilt thou dare the wrath of the Shining Face and His circling hosts? Take heed lest I set down my foot so hard the bridge 'twixt the Gods and Men be broken; then could'st thou no longer minister to man, or strike the full toned chord.

Behold I call the Lahs, the bright Dhyanis—the sons of Law and Wisdom—and He of the Shining Face, all, all to me—They shall decide.

2. Out from his head, his feet, his left hand and his right, sped four vast streams of Fire. They sought the abode of the Gods, and swiftly brought them to the bridge whereon Fohat stood with lifted foot. From his navel came the Sparks which all unknown to him had power to overcome e'en death itself.

3. So came they all, the Gods of the overworld and of the underworld, saying our power to make or to unmake is all but gone. The sons of Maya have taken our might and wisdom by violence. Thou, great brother, may'st finish the Fifth stride, but when thou shalt rest from thy labor and again shalt lift thy foot for the Sixth,—lo—thou shalt be alone. They whom thou now decriest shall be the Gods ere falleth thy foot on the Sixth Stride, and thou shalt not raise thy foot again, for the circle of Flame shall open for thee and thy line of life be cut in twain.

4. Unabashed but with abated strength, Fohat set his lifted foot upon the nether shore of Time. Darkness overwhelmed all living things. The faces of the Shining Ones were hid from the circling Wheels. The Spirit brooded once again.

## Stanza VI.

1. The darkness and the twilight of another Night were passed. The foot of the Mighty One was raised again, and with His torch He lit the faces of the Shining Ones. The smoldering Sparks awoke to life and sought the teats of Suribi, and on the milk they drew therefrom, grew fat and strong. The Holy Mountain woke, and from its depths arose vast clouds of fire and smoke and thunderous sounds. The demons of the underworld came forth and shook the face of the Dark Star 'til once again it stood in balance true.

2. Unto him of the Shining Face, Meru cried loudly, "Smile thou upon my face and unlock the chain which binds the lesser lives in frozen bonds, that so the new clothed Sparks make living things to grow for Maya's Sons to feed upon when they be come again to seek fulfillment of their dreams.

3. Then came the Dhyan Chohans—the Devas of the Fourth—those who failed the Third. Said they to the Shining Face: "Let us now finish the labor wherein we failed; we have learned our lesson." Then entered they the bodies created for them. The fathers of the Fourth became their own offspring of the Fifth. They took unto themselves mates and created abundantly. But their offspring knew naught of their fathers' offenses against the Gods, or the causes for karmic visitation upon them; their minds were holden. Fierce and bitter was the struggle 'twixt them and the nature spirits clothed in lower forms, and with the demon hosts of the underworld. At times they lost, at times they won. They cried unto the images they made with their own hands, and to the stars, and to the invisible ones, "Show us the mysteries of our fathers. We are blind and deaf and dumb before our enemies. We grope in the darkness for the Light which lit the Fire which now burns so low within us. We know that Light burns clear and bright in hidden places, but ever as we draw near to it it recedes from

us. The darkness increases by contrast when we have lost the faint gleam of that Light. Rather would we die than suffer always from the gnawing pain of unrequited longing for that Light."

4. Then awoke compassion in the heart of the Mighty One—He who rides the White Horse in majesty—and He answered them, saying, "I will send forth my Son. He will be clothed in Fire and be as a torch to light the Fires in your hearts. From the Fires so lit will the true Light shine upon you." The space between the upper and nether waters of the heavens opened, and One came forth in power and glory as a sun. He stood upon the topmast arc of the Dark Star and touched the blinded eyes, the ears and lips of all the supplicants gathered there to see and hear and speak to Him. Said He to them, "I am sent to be a torch to light the Fires within your hearts, and I will stay with you until the Sacred Light shall shine so bright that every foe will stand revealed before your eyes, but you alone have power to slay those foes. Go ye forth to gather fuel, and lay the Fires aright."

5. He called aloud and the Great Mother descended with the Lipicas. They cooled and pressed the Fiery Sparks. Where they had been Three, Four and Five angled when the long night fell at the close of the Fifth, they were now molded and pressed into the Six and Seven angled.

6. The Six Sons of Fohat came to harden, condense and direct them into form, according to the pattern of the Chayas of the Gods.

### Stanza VII.

1. The wild White Bull o'ershadowed the Great Red Cow, and with one expulsive effort she gave birth to a Pure White She Calf.

On either side of its head came a Golden Horn and in the middle sprang forth suddenly a Diamond Tipped Horn.

2. Fast grew the Three Horns, many cubits by day. The Two Golden Horns circled the races of the Changing Star. The Middle Horn curved and entered the Earth and sought the abodes of the Serpents of

Wisdom. It drew them forth from their retreat and set them in high places.

3. When their eyes beheld the White Calf they said with one voice, "Thou art a sign to us. Now will we enter the Circle of the Golden Horns, and will give of our Wisdom to those whom thou wilt mark with thine own sign, and they shall be our Messengers to young and old alike."

4. Two new doors were opened from the finite to the infinite. The clear white ray of the Divine Sun shone through the newly opened doors and did not break into fragments. The face of the once Dark Star was changed; it shone with brilliant light. Its companion Wheels now caught the broken rays, for they were last in the race.

5. The Great Mother cried to the One Eternal, "My work is done for this thy once rejected Son; and he shall rule my progeny, while I return to Thee." Then fell the bars between the upper and the under worlds.

6. The Dragon of Wisdom descended, and with it the Diamond Souled Host. In their own diviner essence they enfolded the forms created for them—no longer Maya's Sons were they, but Sons of Will and Yoga.

7. No more shall the bars be raised between the finite and the infinite, for the Sixth shall fall into the Seventh with ease.

### Stanza VIII.

1. At last the Full-toned Chord was struck by Maya's Sons, and at the sound Illusion vanished. Truth stood full revealed. Knowledge, Power, the glory of achievement clothed the newly born as a garment.

2. Adown the star-spangled path of the Gods—the path of lesser Lights awaiting birth in other forms—came One unlike the Gods, yet kin to them; like unto man, yet more than man; One clothed in raiment, glistening like the hoar frost in the sun; majestic, stern of countenance, yet soft of speech.

3. From lesser Light to Light He stepped, and as His footsteps pressed each Star it gave a chord of sweetest melody. As He drew near and nearer still,

each new pressed chord was placed in song triumphant.

4. At length he halted, poised aloft and bent His ear to catch the song the Stars now sang so clear and strong from far beneath His feet.

5. The once Dark Star now shone with glory reflected from His face and full and clear He heard the echo of the chord which hitherto had sounded only minor tones of woe and anguish.

6. The King had come into His own and now was known to them. I am the first, He said, and I am last, and we are one. Out of the darkness hath come the light. Out of nothing hath come all things. Out of Death hath come Light eternal. It is done.

### Stanza IX.

1. From the East, the West, the North, the South come the four Holy Ones. On their way they gather the hosts of destroyers thronging their path, and set them in swifter motion.

2. At the ring "Pass Not" they pause, and with one accord cry unto Kwan Yin, "Speak thou but one word, a word of two parts, and we will bear that word "within the veil" upon our wings.

3. Then with a loud voice Kwan Yin gave utterance to the word. It shook the heavens and reopened the path between the fiery red star and the star which had been cleansed of its blackness.

4. Said he to the Holy Ones, "Gather your hosts and make fit habitation for the Angels of the Voice. They shall lead the new born Sons of Will and Yoga within the path I have opened, that they may people the fiery red star with a new race.

Dongma shall open their eyes to the Glory of the Hidden Way.

# THE STANZAS OF DZJN.
## THEOGENESIS.
### Stanza I.

1. Since Fohat gathered two lines of fire in a close embrace, forming a circle of flame to make room for the feet of the Fifth, have the demi-Gods been filling that Kosmic field with images of themselves.

2. To and fro have the first-born run, darting behind each Flaming Sword that sprang from the head of the Mighty One, while seeking for Pasture against the day of the birth of the great Red Cow. The milk of that cow will gather and flow in rivers of Water and Wine to quench the thirst of the twice-born Lords of the Sacred Mystic Fire.

#### COMMENTARY.

Fohat is the active principle in the Kosmos, manifesting as the outward vibratory force, which thus becomes the creative principle in the Universe. He is, therefore, the Great Breath acting in its creative capacity through Matter. Lines of any character are but the effect of vibration in a given direction, hence they represent vibratory currents of force. The two lines of fire gathered by Fohat are the two currents of vibration set into activity by the activity of Fohat; that is, they are the two active currents of the Great Breath as it manifests through Matter. In other words, they are the Positive and the Negative Principles, or Kosmical Electricity and Magnetism. These two currents were acting through the medium of the Fire Principle, which will in this case represent the Manas. The gathering of the two lines of fire in a close embrace indicates the union of the positive and the negative poles of the Manas in such a way as to provide the proper base for the state of activity which is to be manifested as a result of this embrace. It was this union of the two aspects that prepared the nucleus for the Material Sphere where the Life of the Kosmos was to express itself in the New Aspect. This nucleus was the circle of flame which gave room for the feet of the Fifth. The Fifth here is the Fifth Principle or Manas, and also its incarnation in the Fifth Race. Thus

we are to see that the two currents or lines of fire are the
Positive and Negative Currents of the Manas, and their
conjunction means the creation of a vortex in the Manas,
the two currents acting centripetally and thereby react-
ing upon themselves, creating a centrifugal force which
flows out from this center, thus creating the vortex wheel
of the Manas, which perpetually whirls and in this way
begins the manifestation of the Manasic Cycle, for this is
the origin of the present Manasic Round which is now
coming to a close. The Kosmos manifesting during this
Round will, of course, have to be Manasic in its keynote,
and therefore the humanity living during this period
will have to specialize Manas, for the reason that the
dominant note of the Kosmos will be Manasic during
this entire Round. The Manasic Race is, therefore, the
inevitable result of the Manasic Round. It is not true
that they were souls who had worked out all the lower
principles during the time of former Rounds, for the
idea of merit in this connection is altogether wrong. The
New Race is not the incarnation of the former Race, but
rather the individualization of the New Round. This,
of course, is stated mystically. The meaning is that the
souls at any time are the expressions of the Kosmical
Energy active at that particular time, and not the result of their own former actions. These souls are the
effects of the Round which produces them, though they
may contribute to some extent to the hastening or re-
tarding of the next Round. It has been in this way that
the Fifth Race has grown up during the Manasic Round,
which has been produced by the action of Fohat upon
the Manasic Octave. The demi-gods here are the diverse
Kosmical currents which are acting upon the Manasic
Octave. They mold the development of the Human Minds
and therefore souls which live during this time, so that
they are but so many incarnations of those Forces, hence
they are spoken of as images of themselves; that is, they
are the expression in form of the forces which have organized them. All the entities produced during this period
are the images of the Manasic Forces which energizes
them, and so it must be as long as the present Round
shall last. The Kosmic field here is the Kosmos organized by the Manasic Round.

The Mighty One in the second Sloka is Fohat also.
The Flaming swords are the destructive forces which are
the result of that active force. The running to and fro

is the active life of the creations of those Kosmic Powers. Not so much human beings as the archtypes or Oversouls, that are first produced by the playing of these powers and which are manifesting through the diverse human beings, the Geniuses of the people rather than the people themselves. They are the Creative effects of the activities of Fohat, corresponding to the Devas, only the latter are related to the body of the Kosmos, whereas these are related to the individual life animating it. These first-born, that is the ones coming before man, being the arch-types of men, are all the time dodging the Swords or destructive forces of Fohat, and it is only as they are able to do this that they are able to live in the struggle, for life is the continual struggle between the creative and destructive forces of Fohat. This struggle is in the region of the archtypes and only that which survives is able to descend into incarnation in individual life. They are continually seeking Pasture against the day of the Birth of the Great Red Cow; that is, they are seeking an opportunity to incarnate in form and thereby manifest in life. The Earth life which we see is the field of their activity. When the Great Red Cow is born all this activity will have to cease, for then they will have no field of activity.

The bull is the generator, and hence in a certain sense the Cow is the generatrix. She is in this sense the symbol of Isis and of several of the other godesses who fill the place of the Great Mother. She is, however, in a still higher sense the symbol of Hathor, the Suckler or the Wet-nurse of the Gods. The Cow is in India taken as the symbol of Maternity, and that because she is the Suckler the same as is the Mother, but this is in reality the Great Mother that is symbolized, but remember the Cow is the Great Mother as the Suckler rather than the Bearer. In a sense also she is the symbol of the Intellect, which feeds on the grass, that is the objects of sense. It will be seen that the Great Red Cow is the Suckler of the Next Round and of the Life which will manifest in the Kosmic Field during that time. The color red is the symbol of the physical octave, and hence we are to realize that there is to be at this time a new birth of the material universe. Because the Kosmos is to be born again it will be seen that it must be suckled, and to suckle the diverse powers of the New Kosmos is the function of the Red Cow. The Gods are Kosmic Powers and therefore the

Suckler of the Gods is the one who gives nourishment to those Kosmic Powers. It means a new specializing of the Kosmical substance so that it may be expressed through the diverse manifesting qualities which are incarnated in and manifested through the living beings in the Kosmos.

The milk of the cow, that is this Kosmic Pap, the Mother substance of the Kosmos specialized for the nourishing of the New Life of the Kosmos, will gather and flow in rivers; that is, powerful currents of force suited to the needs of the diverse powers of the overshadowing realm and on a still lower plane of the individual life of the New Kosmos. This milk will flow in rivers of Water and Wine. Water is the Mother principle, and represents the flowing of the substance which must be the means of giving form to all things. Wine, by reason of its exhilarating effect, is the symbol of the life side of the Spirit, the masculine energy which quickens the activity of the principles in man and thus awakens his consciousness to a higher and more intense state of activity, hence it is the symbol of the masculine or life side. The rivers of Water and Wine then show that this nourishing principle will feed both the Energy Side and also the substance side of the Kosmical powers, and through them of the individual life which they manifest. This nourishment will be of the nature of the New Kosmos and not that of the Old. It is in this way that the New Round will manifest a Kosmos specializing its keynote, and that this will develop a corresponding Race in which this New Race Spirit will be incarnated.

The twice-born Lords of the Sacred Mystic Fire are first of all those qualities of the New-born Kosmos, and second the souls through which they are manifested in life. They are spoken of as twice-born for the reason that the products of the present or Manasic Round cannot reach that state until they have been born again through the action of the New or Buddhic Round. Again the fact that they are termed twice-born indicates that they are not separate creations of the New Round, but rather those qualities of the Fifth Principle which have through the action of the New Round been born again; thus it is, as it were, a reincarnation of those qualities on a higher octave. It is this which makes them Lords of the Sacred Mystic Fire. Fohat, acting on the Manasic

Octave, manifests as the ordinary fire, but when acting on the Buddhic Octave he manifests as the Mystic Fire, mystic because it is the medium of union between the Mental Fire and the Airy Principle of Nirvana. These Lords of the Sacred Mystic Fire are therefore the currents of Buddhic Force, which are the active qualities manifesting in the individual life of the Sixth Race Period. Because these Kosmical qualities constitute the Kosmical Oversouls which, acting through forms, ensoul them and in this way constitute the individual Souls, it follows that all that is stated here of these Lords of the Sacred Mystic Fire, these Geniuses, is at the same time applicable to the Souls through which they are manifested. Therefore, it is true that the members of the Sixth Race will be twice-born also. That is to say, the same ones who are now members of the Fifth Race may be born as members of the Sixth Race. This does not mean that they will be incarnated again through the agency of a human mother, but rather that they will gradually change the qualities which they are manifesting, so that they will no longer manifest the Genius on the Mental Plane, but will express that on the Buddhic Plane. It will not be a case of the same soul incarnating in another body, but rather that of another Oversoul incarnating in the same soul which we have had, and thus giving a new soul, and yet it will not be another Oversoul, but rather the same one born again on a higher octave. Thus it will be the same soul born again on this higher octave. It is to be borne in mind that one does not have to leave the body in order to make this change, for it will go on within him, and not without him, hence he may continue in the body and yet pass from one Race to the other, and yet he will certainly be born again. In fact, he must pass through both of these births, the natural Fifth Race Birth and this Kosmic Sixth Race Birth, in one life to be entitled to the distinction of the twice-born. This Stanza, therefore, begins the transition from the Evolution of the Fifth to that of the Sixth Race Spirit. At the same time it shows that the origin of those Races is not to be sought in man, but in the action of the Fohatic Force in the Kosmos.

# THE STANZAS OF DZJN.

## THEOGENESIS.

### Stanza II.

3. Said the Radiant One to the Shining Face: I will cause a shade to cover thee for a day and a night of time. I will brood thy young, and bring them forth in strength and might when the shade has passed from thy face and thou shinest forth once more.

4. For thou shalt shine again with seven-fold light, and the face of thy First-born Son shall reflect the light that shines from thine own. The black and brown shall be no more, and the golden-hued shall awaken from sleep, and rule as they ruled of yore.

5. Fire and flood, acid and blood, shall flow in streams and drench the star with the blackened face. The once bright sons of the demi-Gods have cast deep shadows upon that face; they have stolen the fire that lightened its eyes and molded it into a gleaming mass to fetter and bind their once lithe limbs. Vengeance swift will overtake and cast them into the pit.

6. When the circle of flame shall open again and the line of life be loosed from thrall, the five will fall into the six, and Surabhi's teats will deliver four doves —each bearing a branch of the Sacred Ash for the help and healing of Maya's sons. Fohat will once more cross the line with another and mightier stride, and will draw the downward àrc of the line of life to an upward sweep, by the strength of his own right arm.

#### COMMENTARY.

That which is stated in a general way in the First Stanza is developed in a more detailed manner in this Stanza, and at the same time there are other aspects of the problem presented. The Radiant One is the First Purusha; that is, the Supreme Vishnu. He is the great fountain of spiritual light, the Great Spiritual Sun, as the Spiritualists say. He is Radiance in the highest sense of the word, for He is in fact the radiance of Para-Brahman.

The Shining Face is the Third Purusha, or Ishvara, for he is in a sense the manifesting face of Vishnu, and manifests the Brightness of the First Purusha. In the same sense that Vishnu is the Radiance of Para-Brahman, so is Ishvara the Brightness of Vishnu. The speaking of the Radiant One to the Shining Face indicates the stirring up of the activity of the First Purusha to such an extent that it acts upon the Third Purusha and exercises an appreciable influence upon his course. Not only this, but he even proposes to act so as to bring about certain transformations in the being and life of the Third Purusha. It means that Vishnu is to take control for a time, and in this way subject Ishvara to his will, even to the extent of subduing his brightness to some extent, and thereby acting upon the universe from another center. This can only mean that he is to act upon it directly, and not so much through the instrumentality of the Third Purusha. This cannot mean that it is all to go into Pralaya, for it is stated that this is to be during a day and a night of time. Now Pralaya is always night, while Manvantara is a day. As this is to be during both a day and night of time, it is to be both a period of Manvantara and one of Pralaya, hence it does not mean the dissolution of the material universe in the sense that this is ordinarily understood in the teaching relative to Pralayas. Farther, it is not stated that the Brightness is to go out, but only that a shade is to pass over his face. Now it is to be borne in mind that Ishvara is the whirling, vibrating aspect of the spirit, the Maya in one aspect, which vibration is the generating cause of all the Monads. He is for this reason the personal God; that is to say, the Mask behind which the Impersonal God or Vishnu is concealed, and through which he expresses himself in the Kosmos. It is when those diverse Monads, which are but aspects of Ishvara, take themselves to be Ultimate Entities and not mere forms of the One Substance that He becomes the Great Ensnarer. The Race, then, is the continual playing and skipping of the Ishvara Spirit, which thereby organizes the diverse forms under which the Vishnu Spirit is concealed. This Race represents the activity of the Third Purusha, and the Manifestation which grows out of that activity. The shade covering the face means that this activity and the resultant manifestation are to be checked for a time, and the only way in which this can be accomplished will be by the concentration of a greater power, so as to bring about a greater force than Ishvara is himself able to express. At the same time we must not lose sight of the cause of shades. A shade can only result from the presenting of a dense body between the object shaded and the light, hence it will be seen that in order for a shade to be cast over the face of Ishvara it is necessary that some dense material be brought between Him and Vishnu, the source of His Light. This can only be by the arousing of the material forces of the universe to the extent that they will to a certain extent make themselves independent of Him, and thus bring the Personal God into subjection to matter. It is this materializing of the Third Purusha that is to cast the shadow over His Face and shut out the Radiance of Vishnu, and of course the result will be that He will himself become more material, and will not be able to express His own proper degree of Spirituality. It is only proper to state that this has already been accomplished, for the Kali Yuga is exactly such a time of obscurity as is here depicted. But how are we to understand that this has been the work of Vishnu? It has been the continual expression of the Spiritual through the Material that has brought about this state of materiality in the Purusha itself. It has been because the Spirit has been operating in the external rather than the internal that this has resulted as it has. This has been the inevitable result of the Spirit's descent into Matter, and the material expression for which this descent was made. This descent was an act of Vishnu, and was as much a part of the Great Plan as the ascent up the Cycle will be when it has been entered upon. The Kali Yuga was, therefore, a part of the work of the Spirit, but was simply the deepest dip into Matter, at the end of which the ascent must in the very nature of things be commenced, which will give us the Sattva Yuga. This will also be the act of the Spirit accomplished through the inward activity in the place of the outward activity.

The young of Ishvara are the Monads or Atmas that are generated through His activity. The brooding of His young by Vishnu means that at the close of this period, or rather in the closing days of the period of the shadow, Vishnu is to brood upon Ishvara in such a way as to begin the formation of an order of Monads which will not partake of the nature of Ishvara during the Kali Yuga, but which will, on the contrary, be pure Sattva; that is, they will be the Monads suitable for a Sattva Yuga, though they will be begotten as it were during the time of the shadow. Little as we realize it, the present time of materiality is the very time when the New Order of Atmâs are being developed in the embryo; it is, as it were, the period of gestation for those Sattvic Monads. The passing of the shade from the face of Ishvara is the ascending of the Third Purusha from the external and material to the internal and Spiritual aspects of manifestation. At this time Ishvara will return to Vishnu, thus drawing from his radiance, and will as a result be able to shine forth in all the Spiritual Brightness that he ever shone with before. This will be the beginning of the Sattva Yuga, and the Bright Shining will increase during the entire period of the Sattva Yuga, for the time of darkness and shade is at an end; we are then upon the upward arc of the Cycle of manifestation. It is in the opening days of the Sattva Yuga that those Monads which have been brooding and gestating during the closing of the Kali Yuga, will be brought forth, so as to express themselves in the New Yuga; that is, the completion of the Forms which will constitute the perfect Atma will be through the Spiritualizing of the Purusha. After Ishvara has been spiritualized and made to shine forth, thus bringing in the Sattva Yuga, all the Monads that are organized by the activity of Ishvara will be of the pure Sattvic nature.

It is in this way that Sattva will be manifested in life. At the same time it is to be borne in mind that it will take a considerable time for these atmas to dominate material life, for they must find time to incarnate in physical form ere all traces of the Kali Yuga can be wiped away.

In the 4th Shloka, Ishvara is told that He shall shine again with seven-fold light. This means, in the first place, that He is to shine forth through all the seven principles in man and nature. During the Kali Yuga, Ishvara has been held in a measure of subjection to Matter, but now He is to dominate all the lower principles and at the same time the Atmas are to reflect His perfect light. It will be a resurrection of Ishvara, in fact, which will cause Him to dominate the entire universe, and this is perfectly right, for the universe is but the Form through which he expresses himself, He being the Spirit of Nature in fact. In the second place, it means that the light which will emanate from Him will be seven times as great as that which has emanated from Him during the Kali Yuga, for during this Yuga matter has dimmed the light of Ishvara, but in the Sattva Yuga this will no more be, and the light of Ishvara will shine forth in all its glory because it will be acted upon by the Radiance of Vishnu the Supreme. The question then is, why is it that Matter has been able to cast a shade over the face of Ishvara? It is because the vibration of the Third Purusha has been lowered and in this way the material vibration has been able to gain the ascendancy, but now in the Sattva Yuga the vibration of Ishvara is to be quickened until it is raised above even the proper rate of Ishvara and will in this way approach unto that of Vishnu. It is in this way that it is to shine forth with such a great light.

The first-born Son of Ishvara can be none other than the Buddh, the Sixth Principle or Kosmic Reason, the Logos, for this is the First Emanation from the Spirit, and is individualized in man as the Buddhi or Spiritual Soul. The fact that this first-born Son is to reflect the light that shines from the Shining Face means that at this time the Brightness of the awakened Ishvara is to be reflected in the Buddh, and as a result the brightness of Atma will be expressed through Buddhi. It will be almost an Apotheosis of Buddhi into Atma. The full significance of this statement only dawns upon us when we realize that in the Next Round we are to pass from the Fifth to the Sixth Principle; that is, from Manas to Buddhi, as the dominant note of the Kosmos as well as of the Soul. Buddhi will be the dominant note, but Buddhi will be a perfect reflection of Atma, hence from the very beginning of this Round it will partake of the nature of the next one, and therefore it will only be a matter of time, and that a very short time, before the Atma will entirely dominate the Buddhi and so this Round will merge into the next one; that is, the Atmic Round, when Buddhi will be drawn up into Atma in a sense, and so Atma will have been made the dominant principle of the Kosmos and of man. This means that the next Round must be a very short one, and the Sixth Race of very short duration, for it must shortly be merged into the Seventh Root Race, which will be the true Sattvic Race. This must be the case in the Sattva Yuga; there must be a race which will incarnate the Essence of the Yuga. Now the Sattva Yuga is to follow immediately after the Kali Yuga, and the Sixth Race can only grow up in the fall of the Kali Yuga, for it has neither part nor lot in the essence of that Yuga. Thus it will be seen that the Sixth Race can only be a connecting link between the Fifth and the Seventh, which must be developed during the lapping period when the two Yugas are mixed and contending for the mastership, but the moment the Sattva Yuga has become absolute it can no longer be developed, but must gradually merge into the Seventh or Sattva Race. This, of course, will be the ultimate realization, though we must now return to the period of the Sixth Principle.

The disappearance of the Black and Brown relates both to the disappearance of those principles from the Kosmos and also to the disappearance of those colors among men. The color of races and types is not due to climatic conditions as much as to the corresponding vibratory activities of the Kosmos. There are vibratory forces in the Kosmos which correspond to all the colors, shades and tints and it is the activity of these vibratory forces that produces the corresponding colors, shades and tints. They are to be seen in the Higher Planes of Nature, and also in the Ether, and it is these same vibrations which, acting on the Physical Plane, give to us the sensations of the corresponding colors. When the rate of vibration corresponding to a certain color is dominant in the Etheric vibration of a man or a Race, it produces in that man or Race the complexion corresponding to that vibration. The Kali vibration is black, for black is the color of disintegration, and She being the principle of wanton destruction, will correspond to black and will therefore produce the black vibration in the magnetic bodies of all, to some extent, in some more than in others. This black vibration will express itself in the gross body in the form of a dark skin, the proportion of blackness will correspond exactly to the proportion of the black or Kali vibration that is manifested there. The disappearance of the Kali Principle from the Kosmos as a result of the Sattva Yuga will be accompanied with the disappearance of the Kali vibration, and hence of the black vibration, and there will, as a result, be no vibration in the Kosmos corresponding to the black color, or the brown either, for brown is a mixture of black with other colors. This will mean that from the time of the disappearance of the Kali vibration there will be no black or brown in the Kosmos. This vibration will then manifest in man so that the black and brown vibration will cease to act in his magnetic body and as a result the black and brown colors will disappear from his skin; it will be thus that the black and brown races will disappear from the earth, not in the sense that those individuals will die out, but rather that they will go through a change in their vibration, and will as a result change color to correspond with the change in vibration. Of course this will cause the death of many of them, owing to their difficulty in adjusting themselves to the new vibration, but the fittest will survive. Not only will this change in the vibration work a corresponding change in the complexion of the people, but it will also work a corresponding change in their nature and character. The two races, Black and Brown, have exactly the types of character that correspond to those colors, and when they have lost those complexions as a result of losing the vibrations which produced them they will also lose the qualities which grow out of those vibrations. It will be in this way that the two races will disappear from the earth and there will be left only the white and yellow and the red races.

The Sattva vibration which eliminates the black and the brown vibrations from the Kosmos will at the same time intensify the golden vibration to such an extent that it will become the dominant color. The two colors of the Spirit are gold and white, or rather silver. The feminine or magnetic side is silvery, while the masculine or electric side is golden, hence it is to be seen that the positive masculine vibration of the Spirit during the Sattva Yuga will correspond to the golden color. The golden vibration will then be the positive vibration of the Kosmos during that Yuga, and the result will be that the dominant hue of the Kosmic Spectrum will be golden. This Kosmic vibration will manifest in the principles of the individuals dwelling on the earth, and will thus become to some extent the vibration of their magnetic bodies, though differing in degree in the different persons and races. This will manifest itself in a corresponding change in the complexion to the golden hue. There will grow up a race of persons in whom the golden vibration is so great that they will have the pure golden complexion as did Gautama Buddha. They will, of course, be the positive incarnations of the Spirit. The awakening of the golden-hued from sleep does not relate to the awakening of individuals, but rather to the awakening of the golden vibration so that it becomes a creative and dominant force, and is thus able to manifest its power through man. All will not become golden-hued, at least not for some time after the time indicated here, but there will rather be developed a Saviour Race of golden-hued people, who will rule the world as they ruled of yore, when the Spirit was dominant in the ancient times. They will constitute a Spiritual Aristocracy, which will guide and direct the rest of the world, as the ancient Heaven Born Race did. They will indeed and in truth be the Twice-Born Cast to whom all authority has been given, because of their spirituality and strength. It is not enough that one be spiritual; he must be royal if he is to rule, and in addition to this he must have all the elements of rulership, and this will be what will be manifested in the golden-hued race which will grow up under the fostering vibration of the Sattva Yuga.

In the 5th Shloka the Star with the blackened face is the Earth. Its face is blackened because of the dominance of the Kali vibration, and hence the rule of materiality and destruction throughout its principles. The Fire and Flood, acid and blood, flowing in streams to drench it, relates to the terrible chastisement which the Earth must go through before it is freed from the Kali influence. It is the sword of Kalki directed with all its destructive power against the Kali forces which have the earth in thrall, and it must cut until it has removed all the vileness of the mundane nature. It is the terrible discus which must continue the reverse direction until it has disintegrated the Kali influence, before it can begin to whirl in the constructive direction and thus evolve the Sattva condition. It is again the whip in his hand which shall scourge the rebel forces, which are, however, not in themselves vile, into subjection to the Spiritual Will, and thus bring all into harmony. It is through this great trouble and agony that the new state is to be brought forth. Only through travail is the child born and particularly is this true when that child is the Kosmos which is to be re-born. It will indeed be a time of trouble such as has not been since there has been a nation. It is this terrible period of pain, as travail upon a woman with child, that is to overcome and then regenerate the earth. and which will at the same time have the same influence upon the humanity upon it, that is here indicated. The pain will, of course, be felt by the people as well as the Earth, and they will have to be whipped into subjection to the Spiritual Will, and in this way be regenerated, and then re-born into the perfect Spiritual State of life and consciousness, the Sattva state.

The once bright sons of the demi-Gods are, of course, the Over-souls which are incarnating in man. Because they have partaken of the material rather than the Spiritual vibration, they have lost their brightness and have taken on material qualities, which they have imparted to the Earth, and have expressed through the souls that ensoul them. The fire that lightened its eyes was the vibratory force of the Earth, particularly its fire vibration, which gave light to it, because its vibration was then so high that it was more Spiritual than material and the physical was scarcely apparent. When these Over-souls have stolen the fire, it is meant that the vibration has been lowered so as to manifest the fire vibration on the physical plane rather than above it, and in this way all has been drawn downward to the gross state. This fire has been molded into a gleaming mass; in other words, it has been fixed, and has become a physical fire that has held all things in captivity to the physical. Their once lithe limbs relates to the perfect freedom of movement enjoyed by the Over-souls, their ability to vibrate all through the Kosmos and at will, but now, as they have used this gleaming mass of the fire to fetter and bind their limbs, they are now bound down to the material so that they are not able to transcend its limitations, and therefore are held in subjection to it. Of course, if the Over-soul is thus limited, the same limitations will be experienced by the soul that ensouls it.

Vengeance swift that overtakes them will be the great force of the fire that will come upon the Over-souls, and, drawing them down into the pit of destruction, will disintegrate them, so that other Over-souls free from materiality may be brought forth. This is not vengeance upon the human soul, but upon the Over-soul which manifests through it. When the material qualities have been purged out, the Over-souls will be re-born, in accordance with the new order of things. This is the real Lake of Fire and Brimstone, and it is not the soul but the Over-soul that is to be cast there, though, of course, there will be a measure of the suffering attendant upon the disintegration of the Over-soul felt by the soul. It is also the fire that is to descend upon the Earth, for its soul must be purged of the material fetters also.

In the 6th Shloka we are told that when the Circle of Flame shall open again—that is, at the end of this period of submersion in the pit of disintegration—when there will be an opening in the fiery prison, and some opportunity for expression will be given, and the line of life is loosed from thrall, that is when the material limitations which have held life in bondage to matter have all been overcome by the disintegrating fiery vibration, and the Life Principle has thus been liberated from material bondage, and then the work of the fiery prison having been accomplished, Life is now set free to again express itself with perfect freedom, the Five will fall into the Six, that is the five active principles of Nature as we see them now will have added to them Buddhi, the Sixth Principle, and there will then be six principles instead of five, hence the five will be five parts of the six. All this goes to show that this trial of fire is to arouse the Sixth Principle into activity, hence we have the next Round brought about in this way and hence the dominance of Buddhi.

Surabhi is another name for the Sacred Cow as the Suckler, the wet-nurse of the gods. She is the lactative aspect of the Great Mother. From her teats, this is coming forth out of the channels of nourishment, flowing out of that capacity as the Suckler, will be delivered the doves. Now the dove is the bird of passage between Heaven and Earth. It was the doves at the grove at Dodona that communicated the word of Zeus. It is also in the form of a dove that the Holy Spirit descended upon the head of Christ, and it is always so represented. The doves were sacrificed to the Lord by the Jews, there becoming the passage from man to God, just as the descending dove is the passage from God to man. These doves coming from the teats are the passage of the pap of the Great Mother, here symbolized as the Sacred Cow. The four doves represent the four aspects of the square, and show that the nourishing force is to douse the material world and thus promote its apotheosis. They also represent the positive and negative aspects of electricity and magnetism, and are the same as the Swastika. The sacred Ash is the same as the Ash of the Gods at the entrance of Asgard, the place where all the Norse Gods meet. The Gods being the diverse Kosmic Powers, it is to be seen that this Sacred Ash is that one Kosmic Force in which all the other forces meet, and from which they derive their essence. That is the Sex principle of the Kosmos, and that is what is represented by the Sacred Ash. The four doves each bringing a branch of this Sacred Ash for the help and healing of Maya's sons indicates that the nourishing streams of the Great Mother are to so charge the material universe with the four-fold aspect of the Pure Kosmic Sex Energy that all the people here spoken of as Maya's sons will embody it, and it will take the place of their own individual sex principle, so long the channel of fleshly lust, and in this way the sex of man will be identical with that of the Kosmos, and in this way the union of the individual with the Kosmos will be accomplished through the medium of his sex principle. In this way humanity will be healed of the material ills that afflict them, because of their separation from the higher principles of the Kosmos, for they will be nourished on the milk of the Great Mother, and at the same time filled with her sex energy and that of the Father of Gods and men. Thus they will cease to be of the present order, and will be born anew into the higher state of being suited to the next Round. But in the strictest sense they are already born, for it is this new-born race that are nourished by the teats of Surabhi, and then the entrance of the sex force into them means that they will have reached the time of puberty when they will express Kosmical Sex rather than that which has been so degenerated in the past. But the most important point here is that it will be the sex principle of the Triad Atma-Buddhi-Manas that will be awakened in them and will descend into the material square of the four lower principles, and hence it will not be physical, vital, astral or mental sex that will be manifesting there at all, but the higher triad. This will work the regeneration of man through his sex principle.

At this time it will be that Fohat, the active principle of the Kosmos, the evolving energy, will be stirred up to action and will cross the line—that is, the Line Pass Not, which is the limit of the present Round. He will do this with another and mightier stride—that is, one mightier than any that he has yet taken. This can only mean that he will close the present Round and start the next one. This one will be greater than any that has gone before, for it will be the last one ever to be taken by him. At this time—that is, at the next Stride—the downward arc of the line or course of life, in this instance Jiva and not Prana, in a word the descent of the Spirit into Matter, will be drawn into an upward sweep, the inward rush on the way of return, the apotheosis of Matter into Spirit will begin. The outgoing of the Spirit will be over and all the Kosmos will begin the Great Return to the Spirit, which is its final destiny. The elimination of this sweep must be the ascending of the Kosmos to Nirvana. And hence we see that this will be the end of Fohat, for there will then be nothing but Spiritual activity, and Fohat is the active principle in the realm of Matter, hence when Spiritual action takes the place of Material action, Fohat will be transcended and thus fall into the nothingness from whence he was born when Action began through Matter. This last stride will be made and the New Sweep to Nirvana will be by the strength of the right arm of Fohat, because it is the arousing of force in the material region, by reason of the intense activity of the Fohatic Force, that all the Material Universe is to be turned inward to the Spirit. It is this force that will become so active that it can no longer express itself outwardly, and thus will have to turn inward, and thus the centrifugal force will be overcome by a centripetal force, or rather, having exhausted its centrifugality, it will become centripetal, and will thus flow inward to the Spiritual Center until it reaches the Lotus Feet of Vishnu. Thus it is that the universe will be drawn up into the Spirit, and thus the material Kosmos will be apotheosized into a spiritual Kosmos, and it is to be borne in mind that this is the result of the present material tendency, for the moment material force has so exhausted itself in action as to become a Minus quantity, the opposite, or Spiritual, force must in the nature of things become a Plus quantity. When the outward force has gone as far as it can, the inward urge must, according to natural law, draw all things inward. Thus the active force of the universe must ultimately produce the indrawing of the universe into the Spirit. Though the force acts blindly, yet it must return to the center sooner or later, and the farther we get from the center the quicker we shall return to it, for the reason that it is only when the outgoing force has been exhausted that it can give way for the ingoing Desire Principle to operate. For this reason the more material the world becomes the sooner will its material will be broken and all things turn inward to the Spiritual state, hence the more grossly material the universe becomes the more encouraging the prospect becomes. There is a limit to the Spirit's descent into Matter, and the nearer we get to that limit the sooner must the return sweep begin. We are not here thinking of any direction on the part of a conscious will, but solely of the inevitable workings of the unconscious will and desire principle in nature, on the basis of the immutable Law of Motion, as a purely physical and metaphysical force separate and apart from all individual direction on the part of a God, Angel, Spirit or Man, conceived in the individual sense of the terms. It is natural law and not the arbitrary direction of any one, that is to bring about the return of the Kosmos to the Spiritual state, for this is the rebound from the descent into Matter, simply that and nothing more. We have ground to hope for this return to Spirit for the reason that it cannot be otherwise. We are not depending on any promise to do this for us, but upon the certain results of the fundamental Law of Universal Motion.

# THE STANZAS OF DZJN.
## THEOGENESIS.
### Stanza III.

7. The four-fold Lahs will emit from their loins the germs that shall grow into three-fold coverings of animal forms, of fish and of fowl for the service of man.

8. No more shall huge creatures and crawling things find room on the Rim of the Wheel where dwelleth the Sons of Fire and Flame. The beasts of the field and birds of the air will meet and part in peace, and both shall feed on the purple grain, the gift direct of the Gods. All growths of the under crust of the Wheel shall be thenceforth forbidden, and man shall live by the power of his Will in place of coarser foods. When the Wheel has whirled one crore and a half, the Sparks will embody themselves in a fruit, the like of which no man hath known. The infant as well as the full-grown man shall eat of that fruit, and words of wisdom will fall from its lips, to the wonderment of the Gods.

#### COMMENTARY.

The Lahs or Lhas are the Pitris, the Father Spirits, in the sense of being Paternal Spirits or Forces. They are in no sense of the word Spirit Entities as being the Spirits of those who had once lived upon the Earth, but are Forces which have a generative power which they exercise upon the Kosmical Substance. They are, in fact, not Spiritual at all, for they relate to the realm of matter, and are the generative principle in the Three Worlds. The four-fold Lhas are the generative forces in the square of matter. When the upward sweep has commenced the vibration will awaken these generative forces, so that they will respond in harmony with the Spiritual tendency of the Kosmos, and as a result their activity will emit these sparks of the new Kosmic Life, life germs so to speak, which will gradually grow into the coverings of animal form, that is as the Astral Magnetic and Gross Bodies of the fish and fowl. The meaning of this is the generation of entirely new Life Germs through the generative activity of the Lhas, which as they descend will organize for themselves vehicles out of the material of the Lower principles through which they pass, and will thus appear on the Earth as new Tribes and Genera of fish and fowl. They will not be the evolution of what we have now, but will be entirely new and original ones growing out of the New State of vibration resulting from the New Round.

The Wheel mentioned in the 8th Shloka is what Buddhists call the Wheel of Things. It is that which grows out of the Round. First there is the Whirl in the Akasa, which causes it all to revolve, and there is thus produced the Wheel, which is ever turning round and round. Every revolution of this Wheel constitutes a Round. The Wheel is therefore Manifested Existence, and its nave is the point of activity from which all things emanate. This, however, does not relate to the Spirit but rather to the Buddhic Plane, for all things begin here, though it is, of course, attached to Ishvara in a sense, as all things have their Monads. The spokes of this Wheel are the lines of force which are descending from that point of beginning through the Lower Worlds, until they reach the Rim, which is the World of Form, hence the Rim is the Physical World which man lives upon and knows. The Sons of Fire and Flame are the men who are the products of the Fire principle of Nature, and of the Flame which is its manifesting side. Fire is the Latent Fire Principle, while Flame is its active manifestation. Men are Sons of Fire and Flame in the sense that they are the organized expression of those two aspects of the one Fire Principle. But in this case it is the Buddhic Fire and Flame of which they are the Sons, hence they are the Buddhic Race, which is on the way to become the Nirvanic Race. The Rim of the Wheel where they dwell is the Earth after it has begun the return sweep, that is in the next Round. The meaning then is that those huge creatures and crawling things which are a menace to animal life will disappear from the earth, for now conditions will no longer be propitious to them, and they will in this Round disappear, some of them by being transformed in such a way as to give expression to the New Life Wave, which will then sweep through the Earth, and others by dying out, so as to leave room for those which will be generated directly by the New Life Wave. But one way or another all these creatures will disappear, for they were the outgrowths of the Spirit's descent into matter, and cannot live in the period of Matter's ascent into Spirit.

During the Sattva Yuga the Destructive Vibration of Kali will be neutralized throughout the Kosmos, and hence there will be no vibration acting in the diverse animals to move them to destruction. The result will be that when the vibration of destruction ceases to actuate them there will be no destructive impulse, hence they will not destroy any form of animal life. There will be no anger, but love and peace between them at all times, for they will be actuated by the Spirt of Peace and Spiritual Harmony. The purple grain is a gift direct from the gods because it is not the product of evolution from some of the grains now growing on the Earth, but is to be spontaneously generated from the Earth during the Sattva Yuga by the vibration emanating from certain of the gods, or Kosmical Powers which will partake of the Sattva nature, and will thus emit a vibration partaking of that nature likewise. The qualities of those Forces personified as Gods will be incarnated in this new grain, and thus it will become the medium through which those qualities will be transmitted to the animals who eat it, and in this way they will be nourished and will grow up into the form of incarnations of those qualities. The present forms of grain will not be suited at that time, because they partake of the nature of the Kali Yuga, and will for that reason tend to perpetuate that principle in the animals who eat them, and as all of those qualities are to be eliminated it will follow that animals living upon such food will not be able to survive.. In order that the animals may thrive during the Sattva Yuga they must have Sattvic food, and for this reason the food must be spontaneously generated by the direct action of the Kosmic Powers while dominated by the Sattvic vibration, which will then be the dominant vibration of the entire Kosmos.

The growths of the under crust of the Wheel are such as vegetated during the Kali Yuga and therefore partake of that vibration, and would as a consequence tend to perpetuate that vibration in the organism of the one eating them. They are, therefore, forbidden to both man and animal from this time forth. All the plants that throve during the Kali Yuga will be accursed until they have entirely died out, or have so transformed themselves under the Sattvic vibration that they are expressions of that vibration, the same as though they had been generated by it.

Man shall not eat the coarser foods at all, or not even gross foods of any kind. He will through the power of his Will draw in the diverse principles of the Universe and replenish his corresponding principles directly and will not have to go through any process of digestion at all. That is his Atma will absorb the Universal Spirit, his Buddhi will absorb the Buddh, his Manas will absorb the Kosmic Manas, his Kama Rupu will absorb the Kama, or Astral Fluid, his Prana will draw in the Kosmic Prana, his Magnetic Body will draw in the magnetism from the Ether, and his Gross Body will feed upon the Earth, Air, Fire and Water, or the elemental gases. It will be thus that he will never have to partake of any solid or liquid food at all, but will absorb the elements directly which he may need for the sustenance of his being. Man will thus not live on food, but by the strength of his own Will. He will thus be above the reach of all terrestrial things, though still living on the Earth; he will be the master and not the servant of the Earth.

A crore when taken literally is a period of ten thousand years, and in this sense one crore and a half would be fifteen thousand years, but the time spoken of in the Esoteric Teachings is never literal but at all times Mystical, and the meaning is to be sought and found in Occult Mathematics. 10 is the paternal Scepter, the symbol being the Phalus; it is the masculine generative principle. When it becomes ten thousand it means the increasing of the generative potency a thousand fold, and it also carries the thought of the descent of the generative principle from stage to stage, that is the Radiant One; 10 is the Generator of the Shining Face 100, who in turn generates his First-Born Son 1000; he in turn becomes the generator of Manas, which will become the Generator with power of 10,000. But it is here to be borne in mind that in this particular instance it is the whirling of the Wheel, hence the generative potency is in the Wheel, hence Buddhi is 10, Manas the 100, the Astral Light is the 1000, and the magnetism of the Earth is the 10,000, unless we apply this to Prana. In either case the thing generated will be the Physical Universe, or something upon it, in the latter case the Ether, and in the former case the Physical Earth; that is, the generative potency will act upon them and in this way we will have the fruit springing forth. Five is the number of the feminine generative principle. The symbol is the window, but it means the Ovary, hence the generation of the Egg, which is fertilized by the masculine generative process. The five thousand has the same relation to the five that the ten thousand has to the ten, and the crore and a half is, therefore, the conjunction of the 10 and 5, that is of the Ovary and the Phalus, in a word the copulation of the Kosmical Generative Forces in the bringing into being the new fruit upon the Earth. It will not be those principles as we have them now, but rather what they will be in the New Round, when the Sattvic Period has begun. This is the work of the whirling of the Wheel, and, therefore, it will be all the result of the Round; but it must be borne in mind that it is not during the Buddhic Period that this will take place; it is in the long Round that is to succeed that short Round, the Nirvanic Period, in fact, when the Sattva Yuga will be in full force. It will have to whirl until it has brought about the copulation between the masculine generative forces of the Spirit with those of the feminine side, in other words the manifestation of the two aspects of Ishvara; when that has taken place will there be generated this fruit, as the embodiment of the Sparks that will be thrown off; that is, the generative seed of both the male and female side will act upon the Earth so that it will generate a new species of fruit. It will be one the like of which no man hath known. This is not exactly correct, for it was known once, but for all practical purposes this statement is correct. It is, indeed, the Tree of Life which was in the Garden of Eden, and which John says he saw in a vision in the midst of the Paradise of God, and also in the Holy City, New Jerusalem, as it came down from Heaven. The Greek word there means wood of Life, and so does the Hebrew, and John saw it growing on both sides of the River, hence it was a grove of trees through which the River of Life flowed. The tree of Life, then, is a species of tree and not a single tree. Why was it that it disappeared from the Earth? It is a tree that can only grow in Paradise, because it draws all its strength from the Spirit, and hence all of its surroundings must be Spiritual; it cannot grow under any other conditions. It is for this reason that it has died out, for only in the very depths of a Sattva Yuga will it be able to live. Hence, when the Sattva Yuga has lasted long enough for the Spiritual force to become strong enough, this wonderful tree will be again generated from the Spiritualized Earth and will flourish once more.

Whenever any one eats of this fruit, which will be the Pure Sattva Guna in an embodied form, there will be given to him so much Sattva that he will be filled with it, and it will take hold of his faculties, and though he be but a child he will be filled with Divine Wisdom and what he speaks, coming as it does from the depths of such Spiritual Wisdom, will cause the Gods, the Kosmical Powers, to wonder, for the Sattva man will be superior of all the Gods, being an aspect of the Lord God Vishnu himself. Man at the beginning made the fatal mistake of partaking of the fruit of the Tree of Knowledge, and he died, but in the Sattva Yuga he will eat of the Tree of Life and there will come to him Wisdom in the place of knowledge. The tree being nourished by the Sattva Guna will be the very essence of Sattva, and its fruit will impart this to all who partake of it, so that they will be nourished with Sattva and thus wisdom will be given to them through the manifestations of this Sattva in consciousness. It will be in this way that the Fall of Man will be overcome, and Paradise will be restored to the Earth. However, we must not make the mistake of literalizing this tree into a simple fruit. It is in one sense that, as all things have their material symbols, but above and beyond that it is the specializing of Sattva in such ways as to be incorporated by man and thus made a part of himself, which will give to him that great Spiritual Wisdom which the humanity of the past rejected, when they chose to learn by experience rather than within through the Spiritual Intuition of their souls. It is impossible to speak plainer here, for there is a Great Mystery concealed under what has been stated; that is, all that has been stated is true, but yet there is a yet deeper Mystery concealed under it, which can only be revealed to him who is duly and truly prepared, worth and well qualified to receive the Higher Mysteries. Whoso readeth let him understand. Farther than what has been stated this affiant sayeth not.

## THE STANZAS OF DZJN.
## THEOGENESIS.
### Stanza IV.

1. Fohat has lifted his foot, but halts ere he reaches the limit of his stride. The Sons of Flame have cried to him in sore distress: "The Sons of Maya cannot reach the ring, pass not, if thou shalt place thy heavy foot upon their necks before they reach the Chaya of that ring."

2. Fohat lifts his voice, that voice long stilled, and bids the fiery servants of his will to take his ultimatum to the Sons of Flame: "I will not halt for Gods or men, but this much will I do," Go thou to Maya's sons and strike the sacred chord upon the seven stringed lyre within each one. Perchance it may arouse them from their sleep and give them speed to reach the goal ere falls my foot upon the nether side of the dark stream.

3. Back came the messengers and said, "We cannot wake the sacred chord. But five of the seven strings of the lyre will sound, two lie jangling and untuned."

4. Fohat roused to anger, shot forth a stream of fire which circled all the Heavens and awoke the Asuras on the heights. Swiftly on the wind of their own wings came they from the realms of rest and gave speech to Fohat, saying, "Put down thy foot if so thou wilt and close thy stride, but ere thou doest so, know this, ere thou raisest it again we with our brothers, the divine builders, will have given of ourselves to Maya's sons that which thou wouldst now withhold, and the two strings of the lyre will no longer jangle out of tune.

5. When the first full chord is struck then thou shalt die—for thou are old and thy work well nigh done, so cease thine anger and give some space for effort if thou wouldst prolong thine own labors.

### COMMENTARY.

The key to the mystery contained in this Stanza is to be found in the 3rd Shloka. The Seven Stringed Lyre is the Septenary Nature of man, each string representing one of the seven principles of his soul. The fact that but five of seven strings will sound, while the other two lie jangling and out of tune, indicates that man has only awakened the five lower principles into activity, whereas the two higher, Buddhi and Atma, remain in a state of latency. This goes to show that this is the Fifth Race Humanity that is here indicated.

Fohat is the principle of Sound; that is, the Sonoriferous Ether, manifesting on all the Planes of the Kosmos. In a certain sense he is the movement of the Great Breath, for Fohat, the Sonoriferous Ether, contains all the other four Tattvas in itself in a state of latency. The first sentence indicates that this Fohatic Force is in a state of activity; however, there is a delay, a pausing in the movement of this Force. The stride of Fohat is the Evolving Force of the Kosmos, and each stride represents a Round, hence to place his foot down means to close the Round. This act is delayed by the protest of the Sons of Flame, the guiding forces, which are directing the evolution of the Race Spirit; it is their cry of distress, that is, the opposition of those forces, which checks the advancing Kosmic Evolutionary Force, and thus delays the completion of the Round. The Sons of Maya are the humanity upon the Earth. The word Maya is from the root Ma. A root coming down from the original language of humanity. In Egyptian it is the name of the letter M; Ma is also the Water, and in the Kabbala the letter M is the letter corresponding to the Water in the ancient symbolism. The Water here represents the Water of the Mysteries. The Mysteries are presented in the form of the Two Truths, Water and Breath, hence Matter and Spirit; but it is not gross matter that is here indicated, but rather the Passive or Static Principle of the Universe, the Heavenly Water or Spiritual Substance, in the highest sense it is Lakshmi as the Great Mother, just as the Breath is the Active or Dynamic Principle of the Universe, the Spiritual Energy; in the highest sense it is Vishnu, the Father of Gods and Men. This is the water which is indicated by Ma. Applied to the human body, Ma is the womb, because this is the part of the body where the most important of all the maternal functions is performed, that of gestating the fœtus. It is in the Heavenly Waters that all things are gestated and from them that they are born, and hence they are the womb of the

Great Mother, Ma. Hence this term is applied to the womb of the woman, because her great function is Motherhood. While the name does not survive in this way among them, yet the Keltic Druads had a perfect knowledge of the Mystery in the Cultus of Ked the Great Mother, and the name Ma still survives in English as a child's name for the mother, thus calling her the womb, or the incarnation of the feminine, and hence maternal, principle of the Kosmos, and where could a more appropriate name be found than this? Is not every mother an incarnation of the Divine Mother, of the Maternal Principle? Also the name Mama is the Pudendum, the door through which the child is born, and so we have this surviving in Mama, the pet name of the child for its mother. All this goes to show that the root relates directly to the maternal principle of the Kosmos, and also that it is older than either the Druads or the Egyptian systems, being a survival from a time anterior to the differentiation of these two Races. Again it is to be borne in mind that this same root Ma is the origin of our month May, which is, therefore, the Mother month, the month in which Mother Earth gives birth to the Spring Vegetation. What was the source of this symbolism and this word Ma? It was not Egyptian, for if it was, then the Keltic Druads would have had to get it from them. But when we realize that the same root survives in the Maya of the Sancrit, we must find the same source for all of these nations and languages. The Egyptians claimed to have derived their Mysteries from the Mysterious Western Lands, and hence it is evident that it came from them. Who were those people in the Mysterious Western Lands? They were none other than the people of Atlantis, and as the British Isles were a part of that land, being higher than the Land of Atlantis, they remained above the water when the mainland was submerged; the inhabitants remained on shore and have been there ever since, hence the Keltic Druads were the survivors of the Atlantians. It is for this reason that they have the Mystery of the Great Mother, and also the root Ma, in its diverse application; they have retained them from the days of Atlantis to the present time. In Atlantis we had the first survival of the original language of mankind. In the Ancient Greek Poetry it is alluded to as the Land at the utmost bounds of the World, far beyond the Pillars of Hercules, where the

Eitheopes dwell. These Eitheopes are in one rendition the Bright Faces, or the Shining Faces, but the most primitive rendition is the people who speak the language of Eithar. Now we must bear in mind that there are two kinds of Eitheopes in the Greek literature. There are first a Mythological Race of Eithopes which are identical with the Lemurian Race, and then there are the Historical Eitheopes, the people who spoke the language of Eithar, that is of these Mythical Eitheopes, or Lemurians. This means that the Atlantians were speaking the Lemurian language. From them has descended that Original Language of Humanity. By this it is not meant to state that all the other Races that exist at the present time, or have existed since the Atlantian time, have sprung from them, as some would have us believe, for this is not true. What is meant is that Atlantis received the Original Lemurian Language and that has survived in a more or less corrupted form in these Races that have descended from them or at least in the roots of those Languages, and also in these Races that have derived their civilization and their religion from them. The Atlantians have survived in the Mayas, the Quechis, the Inchas, the Toltecs, the Aztects and the Indians. The Mayas are the oldest of those surviving nations, the Quenches next, then the Toltecs, the Inchas, and finally the Aztects. Now the name of the Mayas means the Ma people, that is the Mother Race, and the name of their country in Yucatan, Mayax, means the Mother Land. By this they claimed to be the original Atlantian Race, and the Mother of all the other peoples that had developed upon this continent. Ma is given to the country in the sense that it is the bearing Mother of its inhabitants; the name is also given to the Earth in the same sense; that is, as Mother Earth. This will demonstrate the origin and meaning of the root Ma—that is, the womb of the Great Mother— which is mystically the Maternal Essence of Lakshmi, and all words derived from this root carry this meaning with them. Now in India we meet with the nama Maya as the term for the Mother and Maha-Maya as the Great Mother, the same as in Egypt and among the Keltic Druids, hence we see that it there has the same meaning that it has in the other languages, and that the Cultus of the Great Mother is at the bottom of all the Mysticism of Hindooism. The all-important matter for our purpose, though, is the fact that Maya means Mother in Sanscrit and hence Maya is the Great Mother. Again, Maya is the skipping and playing of the Spiritual Force, the Sporting of Ishvara. The former sense as the Great Mother is that of the Passive Substance of the Spirit, while this second aspect is that of that substance in a state of activity, as we see it in the case of the Third Purusha. This is the Sporting and juggling of the Spiritual Principle, thus manifesting the forms which grow out of this whirling and playing. This gives rise to the forms which are taken for realities and not for mere appearances of the Mother Substance. Name and form become the subject of our contemplation, and thus ensnares us so that we fail to see the Reality that is taking on all those changing forms of manifestation; thus Illusion arises through our mistaking the form for the Substance and Energy which produces it. This is the sense in which Maya becomes Illusion; it is the Mother Substance masquerading in all those fleeting forms which delude man so that he does not recognize her, and this fleeting Garment of Illusion is what he calls Nature. The Sons of Maya, then, are the products of this dance of Illusion and are at the same time bound by it in a sense. No matter how free they become, they will still be Sons of Maya, but it will be in a different way. They are now the Sons of the Illusion of Maya because they recognize that as the Ultimate Truth; that is they Accept Nature— and are at the same time governed by Natural Law. In time they will rise above this Plane and reach the point where they will become Sons of the Sporting of Maya, for they will be Free from the Illusion, and will express the whirling of Ishvara in their entire being, and at last they will reach the point where they will rise above this Playing and will express the perfect substance of the Spirit, on Para-Nirvana, but they will still be sons of Ma the Mother. However, the Sons of Maya here alluded to· are those who are products of the Illusion, and are therefore bound by it, and fail to see above the veil of matter. Humanity evolves very slowly, and can only evolve while the Earth is evolving with it; the two must go together. If the Earth starts upon another Round before its humanity has completed the present one, they will fail to begin the New Evolution with it, and will under the changed conditions be unable to carry on their present evolution, hence they will all be failures. It is for this reason that they will never be able to reach the ring Pass Not, if the force of Fohat terminates the evolution of the Planet this side of the rim ere they reach it. Kosmic Evolution must therefore be delayed so as to permit Human Evolution to keep pace with it, otherwise it will prevent rather than promote Human Evolution.

The Lifting of Fohat's voice means the intensification of the Fohatic Force until a great sound is produced. The fact that it has been long stilled indicates that it is the arousing of the Force to a great effort, to that which will end the Round shortly, for it is bound to set all the Powers of the Kosmos into the greatest agitation. It will not halt for the Gods, Kosmic Powers or men; that is, this Force has the will to rush on in its path, without reference to the needs of man in his evolution, or even of the Kosmos itself, which needs time to grow into the new condition. If they will not move with the Fohatic Force, it will throw them out of its way and pass on to the final goal which is ever before it. It will not pause for any one, both the Kosmos and Man must keep pace in their evolution with it. The striking of the Sacred Chord upon the Seven Stringed Lyre in each of Maya's Sons means that the Sons of Flame, the Evolutionary Force of the Race Spirit, to steer up the active principle in each of the Seven Principles of man, so that he will awaken all the latent powers within and thus complete all that is to be done, and in this way enter the next Round, when the stride of Fohat will take the Kosmos with them. This simply means that they are to be awakened to the completion of the work which should have been done during the present Round.

The third Shloka shows that it was impossible for the Sons of Flame to accomplish his work, for only the five lower principles would respond, but Buddhi and Atma slumbered still, and there was not sufficient force in the Race Spirit to awaken them and thus make them function through those two higher principles, in this way preparing them for the next Round. The real reason for this is that the Race Spirit itself is suited to the development of Manas and not of anything higher. In a sense the Lords of the Flames are the Forces of the Spirit, but it is not the Lords of the Flames, but the Sons of the Flame, that are here striving to perfect man, and they are of a much lower order than the Lords of the Flame.

The failure of man to respond to the Buddhic and Spiritual Chords arouses the Fohatic Force to such a state of activity that it is here spoken of as Anger, the positive, driving force which must drive all things before it, let the results be what they may. He starts to complete the Round by closing the stride and thus leaves the Kosmos and the Race without any chance of ever completing their evolution and in this way entering upon the New Round. The Asuras are the destructive, disruptive forces which tend to disintegrate all forms, the powers of Chaos, which are ever at war with the Kosmic Powers of Creation. This positive force of Fohat becomes so great that it arouses all these Chaotic Forces into activity. This brings them from the realm of rest, the state of inactivity, where they have been consigned during the entire Life Cycle, and causes them to speak to Fohat— that is, come into opposition to him, for he has started up a force sufficiently great to bring the Law of Opposites into play. The Fohatic Force may close its stride and thus end the Round, thus bringing an end to the present aspect of Evolution, but if so it will cause such a disturbance in the Kosmos as to awaken the Asuras and also the Divine Builders, or Devas—that is, the forces of Destruction and of Creation—and cause them to go to war with one another, and in this way the disturbance will rend the Kosmos and will react upon the Sons of Maya, causing the greatest disturbance within them, resulting in such great pain that the Sixth and Seventh Strings will be awakened into perfect harmony and the Sacred Chord will have sounded in all of its fullness. The two last strings of the lyre will no longer jangle out of tune, but the Sacred Chord will be completed. This means that the entire Evolution of Man will be at an end. The Seven Strings will all sound, and thus all his Seven Principles will be perfected. The Race will thus become one of Free Souls or Nirvanees as a result of the terrible pain through which they pass as a result of this Kosmic upheaval growing out of the violent force of Fohat before the Kosmos, and its Humanity are ready to go with it. We are here shown what will be the result of such a violent ordeal of Kosmic Life; it will mean the travail of the Kosmos and of the Race, and will cause it to pass through the birth throes and thus give birth to a New Race, which will have completed the Human Evolution. This will have to result ere Fohat is able to lift his foot and thus usher in another Round of the Great Life Cycle. The disturbance which will result from the closing of the present Round will awaken the two strings so that man will have completed the work of the Great Life Cycle all at once, and will during that fearful agony have realized Human Perfection, and thus been born into the state of the Perfected Type; hence he will have gone beyond Fohat ere he can begin the next Round of the Spiral.

When the first full chord is struck then thou shalt die. That is when all the Seven Principles have been awakened in man, and he manifests the fullness of conscious Septenary Life, he will be living on all of the Seven Dimensions of Space. When this state is realized he will cease to vibrate on the four lower dimensions with sufficient intensity to manifest consciousness there, and the result will be that he will cease to be conscious of those four lower dimensions, but will live in the consciousness of the three higher dimensions alone. Now to cease to be conscious of the four lower dimensions means that those four forms of vibration which give us the consciousness of form will cease to vibrate within man, or at least their vibration will be so slight as to make no impression upon his consciousness, for it is this vibratory activity that gives the consciousness of length, breadth, thickness and insideness, the four elements of all forms. Man will in this way become unconscious of the four lower dimensions of space. Now, inasmuch as objects exist only in the mind, it follows that the moment man becomes unconscious of the four lower dimensions of space they will cease to be active and will therefore relapse into the state of inactivity where they properly belong. When man has reached this stage of consciousness he will no longer take note of the Square of Matter and Form, but will live in the consciousness of the Triangle where all things are formless, in the realm of Substance and Energy, and not in that of Form. When he realizes this consciousness his principles will vibrate in that way and the result will be that he will be no longer bound by the four lower dimensions of space, but will transcend them all and will live in the Formless state of life. This will mean that he will rise above the power of the Fohatic Force, for it works through the Square of Form. Not only will man rise above it, but he will also change the vibration of the Kosmos and it will transcend the four lower dimensions of space, and the Square of Form will be drawn up into the Formless Triangle, and the Universe will have become Fluidic, representing the state of Pure Mind. Atma-Buddhi-Manas will reign supreme. Matter will have been drawn up and apotheosized into energy and substance; the Kosmos will have ascended to Nirvana, and there will be nothing below. This is what is meant by the absorption of the Universe into Vishnu. This will, of course, mean the death of Fohat, for he is the Sonoriferous Ether in the realm of the Square of Form. He is old and his work well nigh done, for the reason that the time is drawing near when this absorption is to take place, at which time there will be nothing for him to do. His life cycle is drawing to a close. So cease thine anger and give some space for effort if thou would prolong thine own labors. That is, if thou would continue to do thy work in this realm of form, cease thy aggressive force and permit man and the Kosmos to work out their evolution in their own time, for if thou dost not do this, but dost continue to send forth all this driving force, it will only awaken the warring forces of creation and destruction in man and in the Kosmos and will cause all the work of evolution to be done at once and in a violent upheaval, and will thus cause the apotheosis of the Universe as well as man into Nirvana, and in this way there will be nothing farther for thee to do; hence thou shalt cease all activity and thus lapse into nothingness, for the reason that it is only in thy Mode of Motion that thou are existent at all, apart from this motion thou art not, and therefore when thou shalt cease to vibrate thou wilt cease to be. This will be the end of the Illusory aspect of Maya, and Maya's Sons will be brought to the Lotus feet of Vishnu, and the Universe will present the Playing of Ishvara, but not the Illusory forms that have in the past grown out of it.

From all indications it begins to look as though this was a perfectly clear indication of what was actually going to take place. It would seem as though the Fohatic Force is arousing itself to such a frenzy of activity that the Forces of Creation and Destruction were going to rend the Kosmos to its very foundation, and in this way to force it, as well as the Race, into the New Birth, which will complete the Evolution at once, and in this way end the Life Cycle which has manifested through Form, and usher in one manifesting in the Formless State. The apotheosis of the Kosmos into Nirvana seems drawing near, and if so it will be the work of the Storm aroused by the fiery rage of Fohat. The Kosmos will have to go through the birth throes and will in reality have to die in giving birth to the Formless Kosmos, which will be itself again. The whole Universe seems to be getting ready for such an event, and it is for this reason that this Stanza has been given out at this time. It will help all who are awake to understand the meaning of the Storm when it shall break forth upon the Kosmos, and all the powers of Chaos are striving to dissolve the Universe. It will also direct man how to pass through the Storm and make it the means of his higher realization in the end. It was not given out in the past for the reason that it was not needed for this purpose at that time, but now it is given to the world because the time is a hand when the Rage of Fohat is going to awaken the Kosmic Storm, which will turn all the Forces loose and in this way bring about the New Birth of the Kosmos through pain, thus ending the reign of Form. The Whip, which is the symbol of the Spirit that is of the Energy Side, will scourge all materiality out of the Kosmos.

# THE STANZAS OF DZJN.
## THEOGENESIS.
### Stanza V.

1. And wilt thou then make bold to cross my will? cried Fohat in his rage. Wilt thou dare the wrath of the Shining Face and His circling hosts? Take heed lest I set down my foot so hard the bridge 'twixt the Gods and Men' be broken; then could'st thou no longer minister to man, or strike the full toned chord.

Behold I call the Lahs, the bright Dhyanis—the sons of Law and Wisdom—and He of the Shining Face, all, all to me—They shall decide.

2. Out from his head, his feet, his left hand and his right, sped four vast streams of Fire. They sought the abode of the Gods, and swiftly brought them to the bridge whereon Fohat stood with lifted foot. From his navel came the Sparks which all unknown to him had power to overcome e'en death itself.

3. So came they all, the Gods of the overworld and of the underworld, saying our power to make or to unmake is all but gone. The sons of Maya have taken our might and wisdom by violence. Thou, great brother, may'st finish the Fifth stride, but when thou shalt rest from thy labor and again shalt lift thy foot for the Sixth,—lo—thou shalt be alone. They whom thou now decriest shall be the Gods ere falleth thy foot on the Sixth Stride, and thou shalt not raise thy foot again, for the circle of Flame shall open for thee and thy line of life be cut in twain.

4. Unabashed but with abated strength, Fohat set his lifted foot upon the nether shore of Time. Darkness overwhelmed all living things. The faces of the Shining Ones were hid from the circling Wheels. The Spirit brooded once again.

#### COMMENTARY.

The Rage of Fohat is the arousing of the positive force of the Fohatic Will, the driving force, which is aroused by the opposition which is offered to him in the threat of his destruction. Of course, we must never assume that this is an account of the conversation between Spiritual Entities who carried on this controversy in the ordinary human sense. They are all Kosmic Forces, and the words put into their mouths merely indicate what is taking place within them. The resistance to his action which was indicated in the 4th Stanza has aroused all the driving force of Fohat and thus we see his rage; that is, the Fohatic Force stirred up to the highest point of activity. For any of the lesser powers, either those of Creation or Destruction to cross the Will, or Driving Force, of the active principle of the universe itself was an unheard-of thing, and the very effort so to do aroused all the strength of that force to the point of fury. Not only would such a course on their part arouse the opposition of the Fohatic Force in the realm of Matter, but also the Shining Face or Third Purusha, Ishvara, who has directed the evolution of the Kosmos along this line, would also resent with great bitterness any interference on the part of these lesser forces, for Fohat is the expression of Ishvara, hence when they resisted the action of the Fohatic Force they were in reality resisting the Will of Ishvara. The circling Hosts of the Shining Face are the Spiritual Powers, which are the expressions of the diverse attributes or qualities of the Third Purusha, hence the action of the Asuras and Devas in attempting to complete the evolution of man and the Kosmos, would not only be placing themselves in opposition to the trend of Fohatic action, but likewise to that of the Third Purusha and to all of the Spiritual Powers; that is, they will in reality be resisting the tendency of the entire Kali Yuga and this would draw down upon them all of the force of those Powers which would be aroused for the maintenance of their position. This will, of course, mean a war between the Devas and Asuras on the one side and of all the Great Powers, Material and Spiritual, on the other. The threat of Fohat to set down his foot so hard that the bridge 'twixt the Gods or Kosmic Powers and men be broken means that if they oppose him enough so that he becomes angered beyond all bounds this intense force of activity will become so great as to break all communion between the Kosmic Powers and the men through whom they are manifested. The meaning of this is that the vibration of those Forces will become so great that they will destroy any body they enter, and hence man will be unable to receive and express them even in the slightest degree. Thus man will be cut off from the universal forces and will be unable to advance at all; he will be completely cut off from the process of Kosmic Evolution, and this by reason of the fact that the activity of the Kosmic Forces was so intense that it was not possible for man to give expression to it. This would, of course, put a final stop to the progress of Human Evolution and hence man would remain at a standstill until the destructive force of Kosmic Evolution eliminated him from the face of the earth as one of those unfitted to survive in the struggle.

Fohat then calls the Lahs the Father Spirits, those powers that have originated the present forms of earth life, in a certain sense the archtypes of the various lives manifesting in the physical world, the overshadowing group spirits, though they are also material. They are the sons of Law, that is of the Good Law, which regulates all things and of that Kosmic Wisdom, the great analytic principle of the Universe. Law and Wisdom are then merely names for the principles of Kosmic synthesis and analysis, as the two-fold creative and evolutionary process. They are the sons of this Law and Wisdom, as is everything else, because they are all the products of these two principles. Fohat's calling them, and also Ishvara, He of the Shining Face, to decide the matter, means that the intense activity of the Fohatic Force has awakened the Lahs and even Ishvara to a corresponding activity, and it is to be the work of these powers to decide the conflict between the Fohatic Force and the Lesser Powers by joining forces with one side or the other.

The four vast streams of Fire which were sent forth from the head, feet and the two hands of Fohat indicate the square of force which was excited by the Fohatic vibration, so that it manifests as the Fiery Principle. The stream from his head is the Fire on the Mental Octave, which awakens all the force of the Manas, that from the feet is the Physical Fire arousing all the activities of the Physical Plane, and that from the right hand is the positive and that from the left hand the negative current of the Astral Light, now kindled into a Fire. Thus it is seen that all the power of the Fohatic Force is now manifesting in the form of Fire and those streams of Fire are

surging through the Three Worlds. These streams of
Fire surge through all the Three Worlds, and arouse the
Kosmic Powers or Gods and bring them forth, that is
they are aroused to action, and thus come to the bridge
where Fohat stands with uplifted foot; that is to say,
they are now active on the channel between themselves
and man; it is the stirring up of all the forces of the
Three Worlds, as well as the Spirit itself, so that they
are in a state of united action on the path between the
Upper Lords and the Human Race through which they
manifest. The navel is the seat of the 144,000 Nades or
Forces into which the Human magnetism is differentiated,
hence it is the symbol for those Nades in their concentrated action. Now these Nades are all present in the
Fohatic Force the same as in man, hence the Navel of
Fohat is the activity of the Nades. This activity emitted
the Sparks of a Fourth Fire, that of Buddhi, which would
become the Archtype of a new form of Life, and which
will incarnate in the humanity of the next Round and in
this way develop the Buddhic life, which will in this way
overcome death and bring in the state of deathless life.
This was unknown to Fohat, for he despised man, and
had no wish to be of service to him, but his activity had
to produce this effect, hence his very anger was the means
of perfecting the race which he despised.

The Gods of the Overworld are the powers transcending the Physical Plane. While those of the underworld
are those on the physical plane, particularly those of the
Etheric Regions. The development of the man during
this Fifth Round has been so great that there are very
little powers left to the Gods or Kosmic Powers; man
has practically conquered the Three Worlds and there is
nothing left that is not in his hands. The power of the
Gods to make and unmake is all but gone, because man
has evolved to such a point that this power is now practically his.

Man has developed until the might of the Powers is
his, and he has so advanced in Science that their wisdom
is his; that is, he has about finished the Evolution of the
Fifth Principle, hence he is master and not slave of the
Three Worlds; hence he must enter into the Sixth Sphere
ere he finds that which is beyond him. At the beginning
of the Sixth Round man will become supreme, for he
will then be on the Buddhic Plane, hence the Laws of the

Three Worlds will no longer bind, but will obey him; hence he will be superior to all Laws below that Plane. They will be the Gods before the end of that period, for the reason that they will direct the Powers of Material Nature and hence will be their rulers. This goes to show that during the Sixth Round man is to gain through the power of his will complete control over all the forces of material nature, so that he will direct them as his slaves. This is the great culmination of human evolution during that time. At the end of this Sixth Round there will be established the Spiritual Round, and hence the circle of Flame will open and Fohat will be swallowed up in the Spiritual Vibration, and hence there will be no more material activity, but the Spiritual vibration will now assume the control in the evolution of the Universe. This being the case, the line of life or course of activity of Fohat will be cut in twain, for now he will cease to act, and Spiritual Activity will take the place of Material Activity. Thus must be the consummation of the Sixth Round, and thus it shows the way in which the Seventh Round is to be brought about and what we may look for at that time.

This conversation is in reality the contention of the forces of the different parties concerned, and it is in this way that it is impressed upon Fohat what will be the result of his action, and yet he cannot delay, for the force of the Shining Face is directing him to take this particular course, and he must act. He is not abashed by this opposition, though his strength is somewhat abated, being exhausted by the conflict with the other powers, but he sets his foot upon the nether shore of time and thus brings the Fifth Round to a close. The description here given of the result reads very much as though all life perished from the earth, and as though there was here a description of a period of pralaya in the ordinarily accepted sense of the word, and yet this would be misleading, for this description is but a blind to hide the Truth. It is relative darkness and not absolute darkness that is here described. It is a state of inactivity, a form of Kosmical Como that is to come over all things at the very end of the Fifth Round, when the Descent of the Spirit will have exhausted itself, and the ascent of Matter into Spirit has not as yet commenced. It is thus at the point where all action has reached the lowest point, and there is

the greatest degree of inaction, hence all living things
are in darkness and at a standstill. This is the result
of the closing of the Fifth Round, and of the fact that
as yet the Sixth or Buddhic Round has not as yet gotten
under way, hence the new whirl has not began to move
with a sufficient force to awaken the new stage of Life
evolution. This it is that is described here as being
the darkness of death. The Circling Wheels are the
diverse Whirls which are active in the Universal Substance and the Shining Ones are the Great Spiritual
Forces which are hidden from the Circling Wheels for
the reason that all is now chaotic and the Spiritual Powers have not as yet assumed control of the seething world
of matter, which is in a state of chaos once more. The
present order being overthrown, and all things reduced
to a state of chaos, relatively speaking, though this does
not mean that life will actually cease on the earth, but
rather that there will be no fixed character to evolution
as it is now, and there will be a time of dreaming activity or rather inactivity; the Spirit will brood once again.
Matter having lost the particular character which was
given to it by the Spirit during the Fifth Round, it will
now respond to the brooding of the Spirit, which will
give to it a new character. This will not be all at
once, but will rather be a gradual change from the old
to the new Round condition as a result of this brooding.
It is the brooding of the Spirit which is to transform all
things, and start the Kòsmic Substance to whirling in
accordance with the Spirit of the New Round. It will
be seen then that there is no time when life ceases entirely, but at the same time there will be a condition
when its activity is reduced to a minimum, and all things
seem to be at a standstill, but this will be only for a short
time, though it is spoken of as a long night; but this is
spoken not so much with reference to the length of time,
for on the Buddhic Plane there is no such thing as time,
as it is with reference to the intensity of the time of
night; that is, the completeness of the obscurity which
is to end the Fifth Round. It goes to show that there
is not to be left a single vestige of the Fifth Round, but
the Night is to continue until it is all over, and there is
nothing left of it, and all things have become perfectly
static, and can in this way be molded anew by the
brooding Spirit. This period of Night is the conclusion

of the Downward Arc of the Line of Life, and it must
continue until it has brought forth the Return Sweep,
when all things shall begin the return to the Spirit. This
Shloka then relates to the time of the end of the Fifth
Round, ere the Sixth has began to Whirl. It is to be
borne in mind that all this is the outgrowth of the way
in which the Fohatic Force has manifested, for all form
of material existence is but the manifestations of the
Great Breath under the form of the Fohatic Force. This
state of chaos must in the very nature of things result in
the inward motion which will mean the Sixth Round of
the Kosmic Motion, for it cannot stay in this motionless
state, for the moment the Fifth Round vibration has
ceased the Sixth Round vibration must take its place.
This will not be by the drawing of a sharp line between
the two, but rather the gradual lapping of the two modes
of motion, so as to have during this time a slight blend-
ing of the two. It is this process that constitutes the
Spirit's brooding over matter.

# THE STANZAS OF DZJN.

## THEOGENESIS.

### Stanza VI.

1. The darkness and the twilight of another Night were passed. The foot of the Mighty One was raised again, and with His torch He lit the faces of the Shining Ones. The smoldering Sparks awoke to life and sought the teats of Suribi, and on the milk they drew therefrom, grew fat and strong. The Holy Mountain woke, and from its depths arose vast clouds of fire and smoke and thunderous sounds. The demons of the underworld came forth and shook the face of the Dark Star 'til once again it stood in balance true.

2. Unto him of the Shining Face, Meru cried loudly, "Smile thou upon my face and unlock the chain which binds the lesser lives in frozen bonds, that so the new clothed Sparks make living things to grow for Maya's Sons to feed upon when they be come again to seek fulfillment of their dreams.

3. Then came the Dhyan Chohans—the Devas of the Fourth—those who failed the Third. Said they to the Shining Face: "Let us now finish the labor wherein we failed; we have learned our lesson." Then entered they the bodies created for them. The fathers of the Fourth became their own offspring of the Fifth. They took unto themselves mates and created abundantly. But their offspring knew naught of their fathers' offenses against the Gods, or the causes for karmic visitation upon them; their minds were holden. Fierce and bitter was the struggle 'twixt them and the nature spirits clothed in lower forms, and with the demon hosts of the underworld. At times they lost, at times they won. They cried unto the images they made with their own hands, and to the stars, and to the invisible ones, "Show us the mysteries of our fathers. We are blind and deaf and dumb before our enemies. We grope in the darkness for the Light which lit the Fire which now burns so low within us. We know that Light burns clear and bright in hidden places, but ever as we draw near to it it recedes from

us. The darkness increases by contrast when we
have lost the faint gleam of that Light. Rather would
we die than suffer always from the gnawing pain of
unrequited longing for that Light."

4. Then awoke compassion in the heart of the
Mighty One—He who rides the White Horse in
majesty—and He answered them, saying, "I will send
forth my Son. He will be clothed in Fire and be as
a torch to light the Fires in your hearts. From the
Fires so lit will the true Light shine upon you." The
space between the upper and nether waters of the
heavens opened, and One came forth in power and
glory as a sun. He stood upon the topmost arc of the
Dark Star and touched the blinded eyes, the ears and
lips of all the supplicants gathered there to see and
hear and speak to Him. Said He to them, "I am sent
to be a torch to light the Fires within your hearts,
and I will stay with you until the Sacred Light shall
shine so bright that every foe will stand revealed before your eyes, but you alone have power to slay those
foes. Go ye forth to gather fuel, and lay the Fires
aright."

5. He called aloud and the Great Mother descended
with the Lipicas. They cooled and pressed the Fiery
Sparks. Where they had been Three, Four and Five
angled when the long night fell at the close of the
Fifth, they were now molded and pressed into the
Sixth and Seven angled.

6. The Six Sons of Fohat came to harden, condense
and direct them into form, according to the pattern of
the Chayas of the Gods.

### COMMENTARY.

This Stanza begins with the time of awakening, when
the time of rest is at an end and the brooding of the
Spirit has awakened all substance to activity once again.
The raising of the foot of the Mighty One, or Fohat,
means the stirring up of the Fohatic Force to activity
once more, so that it begins another evolutionary epoch
of activity. Out of chaos a Kosmos begins to be formed.
At the same time it must be stated again that this is not
a sharp line drawn between the time of inaction and
that of action, but rather is it that there was a gradual
lowering of the activity of the Fifth Round, and at the

same time a gradual raising of the activity of the Sixth Round; but for a time the Fifth Round was so far in the ascendency that the Sixth Round activity was not noticeable, and in time the Sixth Round activity becomes so great that the Fifth Round activity is no longer noticeable, and this is the time of awakening spoken of here. Between these two periods there must of course be a point where the two modes of activity will be equal, and when each one will be struggling for the mastery; this will hence give us a state of activity which has no individuality and which therefore is in reality chaotic. There is no such thing in all the universe as a state of motionless space, for it is all motion. What we call the time of inaction is, therefore, not inaction at all, but rather a condition of motion devoid of a fixed purpose. It is that condition where energy and substance have no design governing their expression, and hence there is no way by which we may estimate the trend of this activity, for in fact it has no trend. It may as well be stated here as later on that this period is in the past. Many thinkers have observed for some time that all humanity was in a state of flux, that there was no stability and purpose in any of them, that the public mind was in a chaotic condition, and all the bulwarks of the past were no longer of any power to hold man in the proper direction. This state of chaos and intellectual and spiritual darkness which man has been going through for some years is the sure sign that humanity has been in its Pralaya, an event predicted in the Bible in hundreds of passages. No man in his senses will for a moment think of denying that this is just what the human race has gone through for some time in the past. This will mean that the race has gone through a stage of Racial Pralaya. Now it is to be borne in mind that the Race Spirit reflects the state of the Kosmos at all times. being a little later in taking on this condition than the Kosmos itself. The Race Spirit is incarnated in all the diverse members of the Race, and in this way the condition of the people is merely the working out of the character of the Race Spirit in the diverse forms through which it manifests, as the Race Spirit is but the Spirit of the Kosmos specialized for this express purpose. Hence it will be seen that the condition of humanity proves that some time ago the Kosmos entered into this state of Pralaya, and

thus the Fifth Round is already over some years ago.
It must, however, be borne in mind that the Humanity
is no longer in that state of Chaos, for they are now
awakening, and searching everywhere for something
higher and better, there is now the search for Truth, and
though at present the efforts are rather feeble, yet they
are being turned in the right direction more than they
have ever been in the past, and there is such a feeling of
general unrest, that there can be but one answer, there is
a new Race Spirit which is seeking for an avenue through
which it may express itself. This New Race Spirit
means that the Kosmos has begun another Round, and
hence a New Life Cycle has commenced, and this is
manifesting itself among men. Inasmuch as it takes a
Kosmical change some little time to express itself in
humanity, it is plain that this Life Cycle has been in
operation some few years even now. All of the Fifth and
several Shlokas of this Stanzas are therefore in the past,
though in the near past. To be explicit, the Fifth Round
ended in the year 1881 and it was not so long after that
time that the Sixth began to manifest itself, though the
present writer would not say positively that it really began as a distinct Round before 1890, but certainly not
later than that date. From this time forth we may
count the work of the Sixth Round, and we see a corresponding change in the consciousness of the people which
marks the change in the trend of evolution. There is an
awakening of the Evolving Life, and a turning of it into
the very channels which it will have to take during the
Sixth Round, which proves that it has been in the Sixth
Round since that time.

The Shining Ones are of course the Spiritual Powers,
but in this particular case they are the Life Spirits.
Their faces being lighted by Fohat means that the new
activity of the Fohatic Force aroused the Life Spirits
into a state of activity, and thus they began to express

themselves in the new forms of Life essential to the New Round.

The Smoldering Sparks, are the Life Sparks, the little lives which are in fact the units or germs of life, and which have been unable to express themselves in any given direction while the time of chaos was dominating all things, but now the new activity of the Fohatic Force awakens them to life, and as a result these minute lives begin to move and their first act is to seek to develop themselves, for mind you, they are the ultimate germs of the things that shall be during the Sixth Round. They are the germs of life, which will during that round develop the diverse lives or living things, the forms of life for the New Life Cycle. Their first move was to seek the teats of Suribi, the Suckler or Wet Nurse of the Kosmos. Their growing fast and strong on the milk which they drew from her, simply means that each one of these Life Germs must draw to itself the specialized substance, which constitutes the Pap or Lactile Fluid of the New Round, and thus nourish itself to the point where it will be an expression of the Buddhic State which will be the keynote of this period. Thus we have the beginning of a new order of Living Things which is to be developed during the Sixth Round.

The Holy Mountain is Meru, a symbol of the Earth, and hence the awakening of the Holy Mountain means the stirring up of the Earth Spirit. This great disturbance which came upon the Earth was caused by the fact that there is now a New Regent for the Earth, a new Genius born to it as a result of the New Life Cycle. The New Genius is in a life and death struggle with the Old Genius, and it is this which manifests the great disturbance. It is not so much in the Gross Body of the Earth as in her inner Principles that this disturbance is taking place, though, of course, this disturbance will manifest itself in corresponding disturbances in the Outer Body of the Earth, which is the real cause of so many Seismic Disturbances since the time of the awakening, say 1890. All these disturbances are but the results of the effort of the New Earth Genius to assume control of the Inner Being of the Earth, and of the resistance which it makes to his efforts, but they must bring so much pain to the Earth that at last it will yield to the guidance of its New Genius. It must, in fact, be whipped into subjection to the New World Will.

The demons of the underworld are the diverse aspects of its Magnetic Body; that is, the forces of the Terrestrial Magnetism. They are excited to action, because of the struggle within the deeper Principles of the Earth, and thus they come forth and shake the face of the Dark Star, which is another name for the Earth. This shaking is nothing but the Seismic disturbances which have been agitating the entire face of the Earth for some years past, and hence we are beyond that time; it lies in our past. This shaking must continue until the outer body of the Earth has been brought into unity with its Spirit, and thus it will stand in balance true.

The new clothed Sparks are up to this time only existent on the Buddhic Plane, and have not been able to descend into the lower planes, and thus take form. The lesser lives—that is, the Life Spirits on all the lower planes—are locked in frozen bonds, and hence they cannot act in accordance with the New Buddhic Wave; thus they cannot unite with the Buddhic Sparks and enable them to incarnate in lower forms. The cry of Meru is the negative drawing impulse which the Earth assumes toward the Purusha to smile upon her; that is, direct the Spiritual activity upon the Earth to such an extent as to cause the Lower Principle to yield to the workings of the Buddhic Wave, and in this way incarnate it. It is, in a word, the descent of Buddhi into material form, under the impulse emanating from the Third Purusha. This smiling of Ishvara has the effect of loosing the bonds, so that the lesser lives are able to unite with the

Sparks, and thus they are able to descend into material incarnation, and make of themselves living things; that is, become a new order of Living Things, suited to the use of Maya's Sons during this Sixth Round, for the food of the Fifth Round is not suited to Sixth Round Humanity. At the first glance the statement when they become to seek fulfillment of their dreams seems to indicate that humanity was not upon the Earth at this time, and that the New Life Wave was going to bring them back again, but this is not the meaning of the statement. The Race which has been on the Earth for a long time has not been a Race of Dreamers at all. They have assumed a rather contemptuous attitude with reference to the dreamer, and have been wont to boast of their practical character. In fact, it has been the boast of the race that the Age was a practical one, that it had a practical civilization. This has gone so far that the Ideal has been rejected by the entire modern world, and they having rejected all thought of Utopia have gone on in the most practical way conceivable. They have tried to conform to the world rather than to make the world conform to their dreams. Maya's Sons, coming again to seek fulfillment of their dreams, relates to the reappearing of an old order of Maya's Sons, those who were dreamers in the past, and who disappeared without realizing the fulfillment of their dreams. This is not to be understood as the reincarnation in the ordinary sense of that term, but rather as the reincarnation of the Purushas, the Karmic personalities of the people who have lived and dreamed in the past. It is rather those qualities which have been individualized in the past and then abandoned by the Life Wave, but which are still persisting in the Akasa, and which will now incarnate in form and thus return as a race of dreamers, who ever hold before them the goal of ultimately realizing their dreams. The present generation is largely made up of such dreamers, and that is why it is so Idealistic in comparison to so many generations of the past. It must be borne in mind that in this view of incarnation it is not necessary that the incarnation take place at the time of physical birth, for indeed the birth of the body has nothing to do with this Karmic incarnation, hence it may take place when one is quite advanced in life. In the light of this it will be seen that the Idealistic Wave which is sweeping over the earth is but the result of the incarnation in the people living at this time, of the Idealistic qualities of a race of Idealists long since passed away, but though the man passes away the Karma which he makes and the qualities which he individualizes can never pass away. To state the plain truth, the inhabitants of Atlantis are incarnating in this way in the humanity inhabiting America at this time. Not only they, but many Oriental Mystics, are incarnating here, and that is the only way to account for the great interest manifested in all things Oriental by so many people in this country. Much of the Karma of the American Indians is being incarnated in the American people in this way. The White People have driven the Indians off the face of the Earth, but the Purushas of those Indians are incarnating in them, and thus forcing them to fulfill their destiny. Nothing can defeat the working of the Good Law. Atlantis is coming back, and the humanity of the present generation is incarnating them, and they will continue to seek fulfillment of their dreams, not the dreams of today but those of thirty generations ago. The All-Father is just, and nothing can interfere with His wise design. The fact that we see this generation of dreamers incarnating at this time shows that all of this Shloka is in the past and that we are now living in the time of the return of the Ancient Race of Idealists.

The Dhyan Chohans are not to be understood as Spiritual entities in any proper sense of that term. They are, more properly speaking, Powers that have exercised a great influence on the evolution of life, though they are powers that originated in the human race. During the Third Round there were some who resisted the Gods, or Great Kosmic Powers, and arrayed themselves in opposition to them. For this reason they were out of harmony with the course of Racial Evolution, which is dependent upon humanity expressing the Kosmic Powers; but when men make themselves positive to these Kosmical Powers, they hinder and defy the Kosmic process and thus they failed to pass the Third Round. That is, they were out of harmony with the trend of Kosmical Evolution, and therefore they could not pass over and become members of the humanity of the Fourth Round. Now remember it is not the human soul that could not do this, but rather the qualities which were manifesting through them, and which were stored up in the great karmic storehouse of the Kosmos. These qualities were not suited to the progress of human evolution during the Fourth Round, for if they were to incarnate in man, they would continue to oppose this trend and yet they were so specialized that it would not do for them to be entirely eliminated from the process of Kosmical Evolution. They therefore became the Devas, or Building Spirits of the Fourth Round, and thus were confined to material things, directing the operations of the Kosmic Life but being unable to develop the Astral Principle in themselves, though they did the work of developing the forces of the Astral Light, but did so as the servants of a higher intelligence, and were not permitted to enter the Earth life on the physical plane. In other words, they were working forces, and not individuals in any proper sense of that term, though they brought over with them all the qualities which they had individualized during the Third Round. In the Fifth Round these Devas had gained so much power and strength that they became the Dhyan Chohans, and hence the directing spirits between humanity and the corresponding aspects of the Kosmos. At first it may be difficult for some to realize that they are nothing more than intermediary forces, but that is all that they can be. A Chohan is a priest, and therefore a Dhyan Chohan is that overshadowing force which is the essence of priesthood, and which makes of the one it dominates a priest. These powers are in touch with the great forces of the Universe, and at the same time they partake of the essence of human personality, hence they are the mediums through which the Kosmical Powers are able to come in touch with the human life Spirit, and in this way influence the evolution of man. Thus it was that these Dhyan Chohans which are in no sense entities, have nevertheless been the channels through which the Kosmic Powers have directed the evolution of man. The result of this work is that at last these Powers are brought back into harmony with the great Kosmical Powers, and with the Evolutionary trend, and thus they are now obedient to the Shining Face of Ishvara. They now aspire to incarnate in man and enter the world of physical experience, and take up the work which they left unfinished at the end of the Third Round. This will mean that they are to enter human form with all the powers which have been developed as Devas and Dhyan Chohans, and yet with the limitation in consciousness due to their failure to individualize in the human consciousness the work of the Fourth and Fifth Rounds.

The entrance of the Dhyan Chohans into the bodies prepared for them, means that those powers descended and incarnated in the bodies of men already living upon the Earth, their qualities being incarnated in the place of the qualities of the persons up to the time they incarnated in them. It is thus by their incarnation into Fifth Race Men that they begin their new human life, and hence this new type are the offspring of the Fifth Race people into whose bodies they enter, and they are the offspring of this Dhyan Chohan life. It was the humanity of the Third Round that gave birth to that of the Fourth Round, hence these who are the failures of the Third Round belong to a class who were the fathers of the Fourth Round Humanity, and they as Dhyan Chohans directed the development of the Fifth Race, which is also their offspring in more ways than one. Now when they incarnate in these Fifth Race people they become their own offspring, for they are now identical with that which has sprung from themselves. This shows that this incarnation of the Dhyan Chohans in human form must be while there are plenty of the Fifth Race here, it cannot be after the Sixth has begun to be developed. The Cycle of Aquarius began in 1881, and this is the Cycle of the Sixth Round, for the Fifth ceased at that time. The first Lunar Cycle of this Cycle ended in 1900, and it was at this time that the Dhyan Chohans were incarnated in the bodies prepared for them. From this time on we may look for an Occult Race, but who have very little Spirituality, and who have not individualized anything like all the latent powers within them and is not this just what we do see at this time all over the world, but particularly in this country? Out of this is to grow up a race of beings of this type. They are to come through the natural births, and at the same time by the occult influences which we have been considering, but in whatever way it is, this type will multiply at a great rate, so that they will in time become the dominate type in the early days of the Sixth Round. After they have reached this state, the new type will not know what their fathers did, that is what was done by the ones manifesting those qualities which are now manifesting in them. Their minds will be holden so that they will not be able to unify themselves with the past history of the Karma which is expressing itself in them, and hence they will not be able to realize the karmic tie between them and the past. Therefore when the karmic visitations overtake them, they will not understand why it is, failing to realize that so far as karmic law is concerned, they are the same ones who sinned in the Third Round. Yet they must suffer all these things until they have overcome all that karma and it has ceased to be any part of their selfhood. There is now a bitter struggle between these people and the native spirits which had assumed forms below the human, for they refuse to yield obedience to the will of these men, there is thus a war of will between the two orders. At the same time the demon host of the underworld, the forces of the Earth's magnetism are hostile to this race, because of the great development of the lower forces in them, and because of the karmic tie which still unites these men to the magnetic forces. Each will struggle for the mastery. It is the forces of Nature struggling with this race of beings for the mastery of the Earth. The men are striving to subdue the Earth, while the Earth forces are striving to subdue the men upon it, and the karma of these men gives the magnetic forces a certain advantage over them. It is a struggle going first one way and then the other, the advantage being first on one side and then on the other.

Their crying to the images which they have made with their own hands for the answer as to the mystery of their fathers, does not indicate idolatry, but rather that they sought through experimental science for the cause of their condition. Their crying to the stars indicates that they sought the solution through Astrology, thinking that the time of their birth might be the cause of their inheriting this particular form of karma. Again when they call to the invisible ones, they think that perhaps it is due to the magical influences of unseen powers, but they do not realize that it is because of the karma of the Dhyan Chohans that have descended into incarnation, and bring with them the debt of the Third Race Rebels. Their enemies, or the nature forces which are aroused against them, cannot be opposed for the reason that they cannot break the karmic bond which holds them, and hence they are unable to contend with them. The trouble is that they are without the Spirit, for that is the Light which lit the Fire, their own individual Spirit. This Fire burns so low in them, for the reason that the Spirit has never been developed beyond the point where it ceased at the end of the Third Round, and since that time, the lower principles have been accentuated by their experiences as Devas and Dhyan Chohans, but there has been no true soul development since the end of the Third Round. For this reason they are in the material darkness for want of the Spiritual Light. The Light burns in hidden places, that is in states beyond their grasp, but it recedes the moment they make the attempt to reach it. This is because the only way to approach that Light is through the development of the individual Spirit. This is the terrible plight into which they are plunged and they cannot see the way out. The problem is in reality, how to develop the Spirit within themselves. They realize the fact that they have not the Light, and that that Light is for them if they can only find it, and so they are continually longing for the Light. This longing is making them negative to the Light, and thus hastening the time when it will dawn upon them, but of this they are ignorant, and because their longing seems to be unrequited, they suffer the gnawing pain which this failure to realize the object of their longing causes them. We also see this condition in the land. We see that humanity cannot see its way to the light, and hence there is great sorrow of heart, for want of a gleam of the Spiritual Light. This is the time alluded to in the Bible where it is stated that "There shall be a famine in the land, not a famine of bread, nor a thirst for water, but of hearing the word of God, etc." It is this time, when the light of the

Spirit will have grown so low that man will not be able to see his way at all.

From what has been stated it will be seen that there are now incarnated in the world two distinct classes, first the dreamers from the ancient Spiritual Races, who are striving after the Spiritual Life, and who are in reality living it to an extent, and second, the Dhyan Chohans who are steeped in the material, but who are feeling after the spirit, and striving to reach it, but not understanding just what it is that they are striving for. In a word it is a Subconscious rather than a conscious longing which they have for it. These are the ones who are so very material, and yet in material things they have an insight and a power which is well nigh super-human, for it is the focalizing and the focusing of all the tremendous Kosmical power of the Dhyan Chohans that is expressing itself in this way. We are still going through this state to some extent, though what is de-scribed in this Shloka is a little in the past, that is, it relates to the time from 1900 to 1911, at which time the next Shloka begins to be applicable.

In the Fourth Shloka, the Mighty One—He who rides the White Horse in majesty—is Vishnu the Supreme—the First Purusha, or the ultimate aspect of the Universal Spirit. This continual crying for Light on the part of the denizens of the Earth, drew upon the Vishnu Principle so that it had to respond to the desire. Whenever the world becomes sufficiently negative to the Spirit, the latter must respond in a positive way, and thus descend to the Earth in an Avatara, so as to supply the Earth's needs. The answer of the Mighty One to them means that the drawing influence has been felt, and that He has responded to it, and has began to flow toward them. "I will send forth my Son." This means that He will send down an Avatara, for in a certain sense the Avatara is the Son of Vishnu, inasmuch as it is not all of Vishnu quantitatively, for it is only that which is able to manifest through the form of an Avatar. It is the descending of the Vishnu Spirit so that it over-shadows a man and incarnating in him, manifests in and through his consciousness. Now inasmuch as this is the same energy as Vishnu, and is a part of the Vishnu principle, still abiding in Him though it has descended to the Earth, it is spoken of as the Son of the Supreme

Vishnu, nevertheless it is also Vishnu Himself, viewed from another standpoint. When this Avatara has incarnated, the Avatar will have the same relation to the Supreme Vishnu that the incarnating Avatara has; that is, he will be Vishnu in manifestation, or from the other point of view, Son of Vishnu. The two aspects are illustrated by the words of Jesus with reference to the relationship between himself and IHVH as his father, when speaking of himself as the manifestation, he says: "I and my Father are One," and when speaking of himself as the incarnation of a part of the Essence of the Father he says: "My Father is greater than I;" that is, greater in the sense of quantity, because the percentage of the Divine Essence which could manifest through a human form was limited, but they were one in the sense that it was the "Father's Pure Essence" that was manifesting in and through him.

He will be clothed in Fire and be as a torch to light the Fires in your hearts. This refers to the Avatar, for the Fire with which he is to be clothed is the Avatara. This Spiritual Fire is to clothe him, to be as it were his very personality, so that he will radiate the Spirit everywhere, for he will be all Spirit. This influence will touch all who come near him, and so the Fires within their hearts will be lighted and they will thus burn up, and give them Light, that is the awakening of the Individual Spirit of each one, to the end that he shall at last realize Blessed Nirvana. "From the Fires so lit will the true Light shine upon you." This means that as a result of these Fires burning in each one, of the activity of the Spirit in each, the Universal Spirit will overshadow all, and they will be merged in it, there the selves will all be lost in the one self, and so these Nirvanees will sink into Pari-Nirvana. This is to be the ultimate end of the descending of this Avatara.

The waters of the Heavens are the Substance of the Spirit, just as the Breath is its energy. The upper waters are the Lakshmi Substance of the First Purusha, similar to Vishnu the Supreme. The Nether Waters are the Lakshmi Substance of the Third Purusha, that which gives the Form Side of Ishvara. The space between these is of course the Second Purusha, and its opening means the descent of Vishnu the Preserver. The One coming forth in power and glory as a sun, is the Avatara. It is as a sun, for it is the center of Spiritual Light for the Earth, just as the Sun is the center of physical light. It is to be borne in mind that the Universal Spirit is by Spiritualists called the Great Spiritual Sun, and as the Avatara is the descending of that Spiritual Sun, He is most appropriately spoken of as being like a Sun.

The Dark Star is the Earth. His standing upon its topmost arc means that at first the Avatara is only able to act upon the Earth's Spirit, all the lower principles refusing to respond to it. This brings us to the time when the Avatara enters the body of a man and becomes the Avatar, for it is only through the form of the Avatar that the Avatara is able to manifest itself, and thus reach the people who need his help. It was on the night of December 24, at midnight, 1911, that the Avatara incarnated in the form of a man, one who was prepared for the reception of it, not an infant, or an unborn child, but a full-grown man, and one whose Reason and Spirit were developed to the point where he was the most receptive to the Spirit, of any one living, and from henceforth was completely identified with him, and thus became Kalki the 10th Avatar of Vishnu the Supreme, the Conqueror on the White Horse, with the Sword in His hand.

His touching the blinded eyes, ears and lips of all the supplicants gathered there to see and hear and speak to him, means the healing of their eyes so that they will be able to see him with the eyes of the Spirit, of their ears so that they will be able to hear and understand the Spiritual Truth which he shall teach them, and of their lips so that they will be able to speak forth the words of the Spirit, and to respond in the proper spirit to what he shall say. It is not at all necessary that these supplicants should know who the Avatar is for them to come to him; for the moment one feels the presence of that Spirit in the Earth, and turns to it with devotion, seeking for Light from it, he will be worshiping the Avatar whether he knows him or not, as the Avatar and the Avatara are one and the same. This love and devotion to the Spirit will reach the Avatar and will draw from him the healing spirit, which they require. Thus it is that through Bhakti it is possible for any one to come into Spiritual touch with the Avatar and in this way get the healing influence of the Avatara. This will in time open their Spiritual Eyes so that they may see him in the true sense of the word, though this does not necessarily mean that they will see him face to face in the physical sense of the term, but they will see with the eyes of their understanding, the real nature of the Avatar. It will open their Spiritual Ears so that they will be able to catch the message which he comes to deliver to the world, and thus will be able to understand the message. It will give to them Spiritual Lips with which they may declare the Truth, which they have seen and heard. And this may be true without them having ever seen the Avatar in bodily shape, but it will come by reason of their contacting the Avatara in their hearts.

He comes to be a torch to light the Fires within their hearts, that is the purpose of his coming, hence all the influences which he exercises must be of a Spiritual Nature, and those who are looking for one to do something else are doomed to disappointment. He will remain among men until this Sacred Light within them will shine so bright that every foe shall stand revealed before their eyes. Now the foes are the Powers of Nature that rebel against them, and for them to see all of these foes means that they are to have their faculties so opened that they will have a perfect knowledge of the nature of all the material forces, being no longer ignorant of any of those activities. This, of course, means the opening of the Third Eye, and hence of the Buddhic Sight. Hence he will remain with the people until he has caused their Spirit and their Buddhi to develop so far as to give them the perfect soul sight, and thus perfect them as the Buddhic or Sixth Race. While he will open their Sight so that thy will be able to see and understand the nature of all those foes, yet it is for them alone to slay, or rather to subdue those antagonistic powers to their will; for no one can do that for us, it must be by the stirring up of the Buddhic Will, that the forces of the Three Worlds are to be made subject to the members of the Sixth Race. When they have learned to use their Buddhic Will in conjunction with their Buddhic Understanding and their Buddhic sight or seership, they will then have the entire realm of the Three Worlds under their absolute control. They will subdue the Earth, but it is in this way alone that it is to be accomplished.

The order to go forth and gather fuel, and to lay the Fires aright means that this work of Soul unfoldment cannot be done by the Avatar alone. He must have the co-operation of the people. They must provide the material, by exercising their Pure Intuition and Reason as much as they can, by study and by striving in every way to bring themselves into harmony with the work of the Spirit. They must do all in their power to prepare the way for the operation of the Spirit, and thus promote their own soul unfoldment. Particularly must they resort to proper Spiritual Discipline, to overcome the Lust of the Flesh, the Lust of the Eyes and the Pride of Life, and thus freed from bondage to the body and the senses, freed from attachment to the objects of sense, they will have prepared the way for the lighting of the Fires within their hearts. This last they can never do, it must be the act of the Avatara acting through the medium of the Avatar, but they must do the rest, and get all things ready for the entrance of the Fire into their hearts. The fact that the Fire is to be in their hearts, shows that it is to be kindled by love. It is the putting out of all love for the objects of sense, all affection in fact, and the substitution for it, of Pure Compassion to all that lives, and Adoring Love for the One Spirit as the Beloved. This will of course mean the attainment of Pure Kosmic Consciousness, that is the Buddhic Consciousness by all, as the Racial Consciousness, which will be the means of perfecting the Sixth Race Spirit in its incarnation in the individuals of the Sixth or Buddhic Race.

All that has been stated in this Shloka relates to the time since the descent of the Avatara, and was fulfilled during the year 1912, and is now past. The great interest that has been awakened in the question of a coming Avatar during this year, and even the efforts to get together in readiness for that event, has been the result of his presence, and of the very work which we have been describing. It is true most of these people make the mistake of assuming that he will come in the future, but the very fact that there is this great discussion of the subject shows that he has come, for the opening of the eyes of the people to this problem is to be his act. It is plain to any one that many thousands during the past year have been gathering fuel, and as far as they

were able laying the fires aright. Many mistakes have
been made, it is true, but yet they are doing the best
they can according to their lights, and this is to be done
in obedience to the express command of the Avatar,
given to those supplicants who come to him, after he
has descended to the Earth, hence the fact proves that
he has been here for the last year.

In the Fifth Shloka, where it is stated that he called
aloud, we are to understand not an audible cry in the
human sense of the word, but rather the speaking of
the Word, which causes a movement in the Soundless
Sound, the effect of which is to awaken the activity of
the Universal Spirit. It is spoken of as a loud cry
because of its potency, for Sound being the essence of
the Force, the strength of the Force will be indicated
by its loudness in sound, that is in the Spiritual Sound,
though of course it will be inaudible on all planes below the Spiritual. The fact that this cry was a call,
shows that it was not in the form of a positive ex-
pulsion of force, growing out of the exercise of the
Spiritual Will, but rather a negative indrawing of the
Spiritual Desire principle, creating a vortex into which
the Spirit was drawn. It was the wish for the feminine
side of the Spirit. At this call, or this drawing influence, the Great Mother, that is, Lakshmi, descended.
At the time of each Avatara of Vishnu there is likewise an Avatara of Lakshmi, the consort of Vishnu the
Supreme. This female Avatara is related to the male
Avatara as Consort, and of course this relationship
unites the two Avatars as well. The longing of the
Avatar for the feminine side had the effect of drawing
down an Avatara of Lakshmi, but the fact that it is
spoken of as being the Great Mother herself, and not
as being her Daughter, as he is called the Son of Vishnu,
shows that it was only a small part of the Avatara that
was able to incarnate in the Avatar, and that the balance
continues to overshadow her and the Earth as well, and
to express itself as best it can on the formative work
of the New Round. In other words, she does not simply
come for his sake, but also for the sake of mothering
the new Race as well as the New Round. As this is to
end the Kali Yuga, and to usher in the Sattva Yuga,
which will in reality be the Lakshmi Yuga, we can see
why it is so necessary that the Mothering influence of

the Divine Mother should be manifested in the earth at this time. She must give birth to all things rightly belonging to the Sattva Yuga. Now she comes to Mother the New Yuga because, as was stated in the interpretation of one of the former Stanzas, the Sixth Round is to be one of rather short duration, and out of it is to come the Seventh Round, hence the beginning of the Seventh Round must be started in this one and that right away. It is for this reason that the Mother influence must be so prominent at this particular time. We are to consider both the Mother Avatar and also the workings of the Mother Avatara outside of her form.

Not only does the Great Mother descend, but also the Lipicas. Now it is to be borne in mind that the Great Mother is the substance of the Spirit, symbolized by water, just as the Father is the energy of the Spirit, symbolized by the Breath. She is the plastic substance out of which all things have been formed, and in this way becomes the former, the molder, the one giving form, just as the Father is the inspirer and life giver. It is to do this work for the present and for the next Round that the Mother has descended. The Lipicas that descend with her are the molding forces that are her agents, the form producing influences that abide in her and give expression to her molding tendency. It is they that work on the external, as she does on the internal side of all spiritual things. However, they do not act on any plane below the Spiritual, hence all the forming that they are able to do will be on the Spiritual plane, dealing with the Monads.

The Fiery Sparks are the soul sparks, which are partly on the Nirvanic and partly on the Buddhic Plane. They are the Sparks of the Life which is to manifest during the Sixth and the Seventh Rounds. The Great Mother and her serving Lipicas cool and press these sparks; that is, they lower their vibration so that they will be able to assume their proper forms, and then they press them into those forms.

During the long night, which was not long in point of time, but only in the completeness of the extinction of the Fifth Round influence, the soul sparks were three, four and five angled; that is, they belonged to people of the Third, Fourth and Fifth Races. It will not do to assume that all the humanity on the Earth at the close of the Fifth Round were members of the Fifth Race. There were still many Third Race people, who had not even evolved an emotional consciousness, many Fourth Round people who were living on the emotional plane as well as many Fifth Race people who had the pure intellectual or manasic consciousness! At the same time there were some who had the Buddhic consciousness, and hence were already members of the Sixth Race. All these soul sparks are now being acted upon by these molding influences, and are thereby being molded and pressed into Sixth and Seven Angled Forms; that is, they are being mothered and thereby molded into the form of the Sixth and some of them into the Seventh Race people. Bear in mind this is going on at the same time; that is, there are Sixth Race people and Seventh Race people being formed at the same time. Not only is this influence being exercised upon the soul sparks in human incarnation at this time, but also upon all those karmic personalities that have not incarnated as yet. They are being acted upon directly and so are all the monads, and the result will be that when these incarnate they will belong to the Sixth and Seventh Races, and thus they will continue to do so after their incarnation. The fact that both processes are going on at the same time, shows that the nucleus of the Seventh Race is to be developed among the Sixth, and thus help on the time of the Seventh Round. It is in this way that the Sattva Yuga is to be in reality given birth to by the Great Mother, for she must bear a new Ishvara or Third Purusha, free from all the influence of Kali, which the present one is not. This will show the function of the Great Mother as the Bearing Mother of each member of both the Sixth and also the Seventh Race, and at the same time as the Bearing Mother of the Third Purusha itself, and also of the Sattva Yuga. The Lipicas are the nurses that assist her in this work of giving form to them. All must be born again in this way, both those now born and also those not as yet born.

The descent of the Great Mother as an Avatara took place in the latter part of the month of January, 1912, and after this, however, it was some little time before the complete Avatara was able to manifest in the Earth. The molding work of the Great Mother and of the

Lipicas indicated above, began in the Spring of that year, and has been going on all the time since then. Hence it is to be seen that all taught in this Shloka is applicable to the present time, though of course it will also be for some time in the future.

In the Sixth Shloka the Six Sons of Fohat are the manifestations of the Fohatic Force on each of the Six aspects of nature over which he exercises control. As Fohat is material force, he does not exist in the Spirit, but only in the other Six principles of nature. These Six Sons are therefore the active principles pertaining to each of those principles. These Forces act upon the Newly Formed Sparks, and so harden, condense and direct them into form, that is to say, they are by this activity enabled to incarnate in all the diverse principles, so as to manifest their own nature through the physical form. It is the descent into matter, including physical form, of these soul sparks, thus originating the Sixth and Seventh Races of men, that is here indicated by the work of the Six Sons of Fohat, but it is to be according to the pattern of the Chaya of the Gods, for at this time men are to become Gods as it were, for they are to incarnate the perfections of all these great Kosmical Powers, and in this way fill up their Chayas, incarnating this fulness, and in this way becoming the Gods in form. It is for this reason that it was stated to Fohat that during the Sixth Round men would be the Gods. The Gods are Kosmic Powers, but when those powers are fully incarnate in men those men will of course be the Gods which are manifesting in and through them. At the same time these men will be in possession of Spiritual Powers and Knowledge which will make them superior to all the Gods, with the exception of the Purushas. They will be what the Gods have been, and in fact what the Gods were destined to be, and will direct their actions, and those of the Great Powers, by their own wills, and in this way will they be the culminating Race of the Kosmos.

It may be stated that this work also has already commenced, and that we see it, that is the work of the Six Sons of Fohat in operation every day. Of course we are just in the beginning of the work, and therefore we must not look for very much in the way of results as yet, but the process is in operation, and will so continue until it has perfected the work indicated. This is the meaning of the Sixth Shloka.

## THE STANZAS OF DZJN.

## THEOGENESIS.

### Stanza VII.

1. The wild White Bull o'ershadowed the Great Red Cow, and with one expulsive effort she gave birth to a Pure White She Calf.

On either side of its head came a Golden Horn and in the middle sprang forth suddenly a Diamond Tipped Horn.

2. Fast grew the Three Horns, many cubits by day. The Two Golden Horns circled the races of the Changing Star. The Middle Horn curved and entered the Earth and sought the abodes of the Serpents of Wisdom. It drew them forth from their retreat and set them in high places.

3. When their eyes beheld the White Calf they said with one voice, "Thou art a sign to us. Now will we enter the Circle of the Golden Horns, and will give of our Wisdom to those whom thou wilt mark with thine own sign, and they shall be our Messengers to young and old alike."

4. Two new doors were opened from the finite to the infinite. The clear white ray of the Divine Sun shone through the newly opened doors and did not break into fragments. The face of the once Dark Star was changed; it shone with brilliant light. Its companion Wheels now caught the broken rays, for they were last in the race.

5. The Great Mother cried to the One Eternal, "My work is done for this thy once rejected Son; and he shall rule my progeny, while I return to Thee." Then fell the bars between the upper and the under worlds.

6. The Dragon of Wisdom descended, and with it the Diamond Souled Host. In their own diviner essence they enfolded the forms created for them— no longer Maya's Sons were they, but Sons of Will and Yoga.

*7.* No more shall the bars be raised between the finite and the infinite, for the Sixth shall fall into the Seventh with ease.

COMMENTARY.

The Bull is at all times the symbol of the Generator, and a White Bull would be the Generative potency of the Spirit. The fact that in the First Shloka he is spoken of as the Wild White Bull, indicates that he is not a part of the world; that is, it is the Universal Spirit as the Spiritual Generator. It is this Spirit as the Dynamic Energy which acts upon all substance and fecundates it.

The Cow is, of course, the Generatrix, as well as the Wet-nurse, but in this instance she represents the Generatrix, the Bearer. Red being the lowest color in the spectrum, it becomes the symbol of the physical. The Great Red Cow is therefore Matter, taken as the Static Substance, which must be energized by the Dynamic Energy before it can act. It is in this sense feminine, while the Dynamic Spiritual Energy is for that reason masculine. The overshadowing means that this static substance of Matter is energized by the Dynamic Energy of the Spirit. This indicates a great change in the relation of things. In the past Matter has been active, and has kept down the activity of the Spirit, but now it is perfectly passive, and responds to the Dynamic influence of the Spiritual Energy.

The result of those perfect fecundations of Matter by Spirit will, of course, be a new Material Kosmos. The Calf will, of course, be this because the Cow is Material substance, and the Bull Spiritual Energy, hence that which results from the energizing of Static Material substance will be an organized form of that Material substance, and this will be a Material Kosmos. The sex of the Calf shows that this is what it is, for as it is feminine it must relate to the substance side, and hence to the material. The color of the Calf being White, the color of the Spirit indicates the Spiritualizing of Matter, that is the organization of a Material Kosmos which will be the expression of the fullness of the Spirit. This is in fact to be the result of the conjunction here indicated. The material Universe is to be born again, and this time it will be in harmony with the Spirit. This will be the special work of the Sixth Round. In fact the overshadowing of the Red Cow has already taken place, and the New Kosmos is in process of development, and soon it will be born. As a result of this work, we may look for many disturbances both in the Kosmos and among men for some little time in the future, because while the change is going on there will be disturbances.

The Two Golden Horns are the two powers of the Spirit, both of them masculine, for otherwise they would not be Golden. They are the powers of the masculine Spirit, which are the boundaries of all things, and they hold the Kosmos in position. They are in reality the positive and the negative poles of the Spirit, between which the New Kosmos is to be maintained. The Diamond-tipped Horn is that power which grows out of the equilibrium of the two forces. It is the balance between the positive and the negative forces of the Spirit. It is this union of the two forces that gives it the diamond tip, which is able to go anywhere, for there is nothing that is able to stand before it. This is to indicate the power of the Spirit in the New Kosmos. It both holds all things in its embrace and at the same time drives all things before it.

In the Third Shloka the great rapidity of growth on the part of the horns, shows that it will be a very short time after the birth of the New Kosmos before these Spiritual Powers will have assumed complete control, that, as has been stated so often before, the Sixth Round will be completed in a very short time. It will only take the Spiritual Powers a short time to gain complete control over the Kosmos, and when they have done this, the Seventh Round will begin shortly. The Changing Star is the Earth, so called because during the Sixth Round it is ceasing to be Dark, and is becoming Bright under the influence of the Spirit. When it is stated that the two Golden Horns circle the races of the Changing Star, we are to understand that the Sixth Race is to be embraced by the two poles of the Spirit, and in this way to be developed into the Seventh or the Spiritual Race.

The middle horn, which is the unified force of the two Spiritual currents, permeates the structure of the Earth, so that all of its principles are spiritualized and thus the Earth begins the ascent to the Spiritual state. In this way the Serpents of Wisdom are discovered. These serpents of Wisdom are the Natural Laws which govern all the workings of nature, and to seek them is to liberate them and make them a part of the New Era and at the same time of the knowledge of mankind. In the Esoteric sense, a serpent is at all times a current of force, and the serpents of Wisdom are therefore the currents of Force, which are Wisdom; that is, they are the Kosmic Laws which for all time in the past have been hidden to man, but are now to be brought forth into activity and into his consciousness.

When they are set in high places, it means that these Laws which in the past have governed the Descent of the Spirit into Matter, will now reverse their action and will accomplish the ascent of Matter into Spirit. It is the turning of the downward arc into an upward sweep to the Center. The same forces which have governed the downward involution will now govern the upward evolution. We have then at this time the changing of the trend of evolution, and in the light of what we learned in the interpretation of one of the earlier Stanzas, it is to be seen that this turning of the Downward Arc into an upward sweep, is to be in the beginning of the Sixth Round, hence the setting of the Serpents of Wisdom on High will be in the first years of this Round, because that is to be the means of changing the trend of this evolution, hence the upward sweep will not commence until after the Serpents of Wisdom have been placed on High by the action of the United Spiritual Powers. This will mark the turning of the evolutionary trend, for the reason that it will mark the changing of the course in which the Great Kosmic Laws operate. This will be accomplished in 1914. This enables us to trace the development of the Sixth Round with comparative accuracy.

When their eyes beheld the White Calf, that is to say, the moment these great forces were elevated and began the ascent, they began to operate in the New Spiritualized Kosmos. There was now a distinction between their activity and what it had been during the time of the Old Kosmos, and they acted differently. Their crying with one voice means that this was a concerted movement on the part of those Laws and that they did not act separately. It was a spontaneous response of all these Forces to the New State of the Kosmos, so that they began the work of Kosmical and Racial evolution in accordance with the New Spiritual condition. It was a sign unto them, for the reason that it showed to them the work which they must do. It was the pattern for the entire evolutionary work, and showed them the way in which they must do their work, the course in which they must operate. Their entrance into the circle of the Golden Horns means that they were to operate throughout the entire range of the New Kosmos, but between the two Spiritual Poles, hence these Kosmic Laws are to be responsible to the positive and negative currents of the Spirit, therefore all Kosmical action will be dominated by the Spirit. This is the way in which the Sixth Round is to be merged into the Seventh.

Those the Calf is to mark with its own sign are the members of the Sixth Race, who will be marked with the sign of the Sixth Round Kosmos, for they are the proper people for that Round, partaking of its essence. These Laws and Forces will so operate in the diverse principles of these Sixth Race people as to manifest in their consciousness a knowledge of their nature and action. As a result there will be no material law which is not perfectly understood by this Race. They will know all things pertaining to the Material Kosmos. This is to be the characteristic element in these Sixth Race people. Where all others have been blindly dominated by Natural Law, they will understand the deepest workings of these Laws, and will intelligently use them for their own development, and for the control of Nature, which will now be made subject to them, and no longer dominate them. It is in this way that these Laws are to give of their Wisdom to mankind. When they are so operating in man that he is conscious of all their workings, and knows their exact nature and boundaries, he will be in possession of all their wisdom, it is this that will give to him his great wisdom.

It will not be anything like all the people of the Sixth Round who at its beginning will be members of the Sixth Race. The majority will still be of the Fifth and there will be many on the way between the Fifth and Sixth Race Types. This is why those Sixth Race people,

that is those who have perfected the work of the Sixth
Round, and who thus have the Wisdom of the Serpents
of Wisdom, are to be constituted their messengers to
those others who have not gone so far as yet. The young
are the ones who have just begun the work of transition from the Fifth to the Sixth Race, and the Old
are the ones who are farther along. But in either case
they require instruction to enable them to realize the
Racial Type. It is the function of those who have finished the work of the Round to instruct the others in
the Wisdom which they have received at First Hand,
and in this way, through their intellect, elevate them
to the point where they also will receive the Wisdom
direct. To be their Gurus in a word. The time for this
Shloka is the same as that of the Third; that is, from
now on to 1914. In fact there are some who have already received of that Wisdom and are giving it to the
other people.

In the Fourth Shloka the two new doors that were
opened from the finite to the infinite, are the opening
of the way for the positive and the negative currents
of the Spirit to flow down into the material universe.
Up to this time they have only been able to act upon
the outmost boundaries of the Kosmos, but now they
are able to permeate the entire Kosmic Substance, and
thus energize it with Spiritual Light. The Divine Sun
is another name for the Universal Spirit, being the same
as the Great Spiritual Sun of the Spiritualists, and is
equivalent to the First Purusha in the highest sense.
The White Ray is known to contain within itself all the
Prismatic Rays, it being the function of the Prism to
divide it into those diverse colors. This White Ray of
the Divine Sun is the Pure Spiritual Ray, which is
broken up into fragments; that is, into the diverse
Prismatic Rays, and becomes the diverse principles of
the Kosmos. It is this dividing of the White Ray into
its seven constituent rays, that marks the division of
the Spirit into the seven principles manifesting in the
Kosmos. In the past the only way that it has been
possible for the Spirit to act in the Kosmos, has been
for it to divide itself, or break up into those fragments,
and in this way act as the diverse material forces. Even
in the early days of the Sixth Round this is the case,
but now there is to be a change. These doors make it

possible for the Ray to shine through the Kosmos without meeting with the resistance calculated to break it up into fragments, hence this Pure White Ray; that is, the force of the Pure Spirit permeates the entire substance of the Buddhic Kosmos, and begins the work of transforming it into a Spiritual Kosmos.

As a result of this Spiritual influence the face of the Once Dark Star, that is, the Earth, is changed. Its materiality is purged away. It is lifted so far on the way of return to Spirit, that it now shines with brilliant light. It is now merging toward the state of Spirituality, when the materiality which dominates it will be a thing of the past. In fact it is very closely identified with the One Spirit at this very time.

The companion Wheels are the Whirls of energy and substance which have not caught up with the Earth. In a sense they are the Planets, and in another sense they are the Vortex rings that have not as yet organized forms. But all the Whirls of Nebulae are included. The Earth having ceased to make use of these fragments or broken rays, as it is now permeated by the Pure White Ray of the Spirit, these Whirls and undeveloped forms will gather up all those Rays, and in this way accomplish the same evolution that the Earth has gone through, and in this way complete their task, so that they also may receive the Pure White Ray of the Spirit. As all the other Rays will be shining upon them now, they will soon finish their material evolution and be ready for the Spiritual Ray.

The shining forth of this Pure White Ray of the Spirit, and its permeation of the Earth, will be in 1919, when the second Lunar Cycle of the Sixth Round has come to an end, and the third cycle has begun. At that time all that is indicated in this Shloka will be fulfilled.

In the Fifth Shloka the One Eternal is Vishnu the Supreme, and of course the Great Mother is the Lakshmi Avatara described in the Shlokas before. The cry to him indicates that she is turning from the Earth to the Realms Above, and thus the current is turning backward to Him. She is already withdrawing from the world, and entering the Ocean of Milk once more. At first one is likely to be misled by the expression, "Thy

once rejected Son.'' He can be none other than the
10th Avatara, and the Avatar through which He manifests. Are we to understand from this that Vishnu the
Supreme has rejected the Avatara? By no means. It
is not Vishnu that has rejected Him, but the world and
its humanity. We must bear in mind that the same
Avatara has incarnated in all of the Avatars. Do not
be misled by this into the assumption that it is the
same Entity that has incarnated from time to time, for
there has no entity incarnated at all. Each Avatar up
to the time of the descent of the Avatara is a separate
and distinct individual, having no connection whatsoever to do with the personalities of the other Avatars.
But it is the same Spirit that overshadows them all,
hence there is but one Avatara in the true sense of the
word; that is, there is one Spirit which descends from
time to time, and incarnates in the diverse individuals,
thus making of them Avatars. At first sight it may be
stated that the people have never rejected an Avatar.
But this would not be true. Of course they have
acknowledged many of them as Avatars, but if they
had permitted the Avatar to do what he wished to do,
that is to manifest the Pure Spirit through them, they
would have attained Nirvana even then. But they resisted the Spirit, and hence the Avataras were a failure
in so far as the ultimate design was concerned, though
of course they have each given to mankind a new impulse, and in this way have directed evolution anew.
It is because of this failure in the accomplishment of
their ultimate design that they have each returned to
the Ocean of Milk from whence they came, and the
Avatars have died. This was the case with all the older
Avataras, and it was true in the case of Rama. The
Myth about Krishna being slain by an arrow shot by
a hunter who mistook his foot for a Deer in reality
shows the truth, for it is the failure of man to understand the Avatar, that causes his mission to be a failure,
and in this way causes the Avatara to leave him. Gautama passed away with that kind of passing away that
leaves not a root behind, because there were none of his
disciples able to digest the Dried Boer's Flesh; that is,
understand the Mystic Third Vehicle. And so it has
been all the time, in their ignorance humanity has rejected the Avatara on every occasion, and knew not

what they did. It is in this sense that the 10th Avatara
is Vishnu's once rejected Son; that is, the Avatara so
many times rejected by humanity in their ignorance.
But now, as Kalki the 10th Avatar, he will not be rejected, for the Great Mother has so mothered the Sixth
Race that they are able to understand him and so have
accepted his mission, and by bending all their efforts to
the work have perfected their Buddhi, and thus finished
the evolution of the Sixth Round. It is for this reason
that the Great Mother has nothing farther to do. The
Sixth Race have all been born and suckled, and they
must now develop as an adult race, and not as children. He shall rule her progeny, the Race which she
has mothered. That is, he is to be the Manu of the New
Race, creating their type, and directing them in their
farther evolution. This relates partly to Kalki himself
and partly to the Avatara. In the latter case it will
be by the individual members of the Race incarnating
the Avatara, and hence becoming in a certain sense
Avatars themselves. It is in this way that they will
pass from the Sixth to the Seventh Race. The Avatara
abiding in each one will rule him, and it will be the
same Spirit ruling then as ruled while they were obeying
the Avatar. Farther it will be the Avatar, for he and
the Avatara are identical, he being but the Form through
which the Avatara is able to manifest. At the same
time the Avatara will rule over those who have not as
yet incarnated the Avatara. This may at first seem to
contradict the teaching that he is to make Moru Manu,
and thus leave the world, but there is no contradiction
at all. In the first place, when Moru rules he will do
so as the Agent of Kalki. At the same time he will
merely carry out the same work which was started by
Kalki, and in fact it will be the Spirit of Kalki ruling
through him, but the all-important thing to be borne
in mind is that it is not so much the rule of the man,
the Avatar, as that of the Avatara, the Spirit which
works through him that counts. So in any case it is
the rule of the Avatara, and it is that is the
Son of the One Eternal. Besides, at this time Kalki
will no longer be suited to rule, for he will have become feminine, as the name shows, and will have become Divine in the Sense of Pari-Brahman, and in fact
an Avatara of El Shadai, and the Seed Manu of the

Divine Race, and the Root Manu of the Seventh Root
Race which is now beginning to be formed. Remember
the prophecy in the Bible that the time shall come that
the plowmen shall overtake the reapers. This means
that the work of reaping the final members of the Divine
Race shall be going on at the same time that the break-
ing up of the ground is going on for the Seventh Root
Race, and therefore we are not so far at this time from
the end of the Sixth Round and the death of Fohat.
This will be the time of Harvest as well as the time of
the planting of the new crop. This will in a word be
the time of the lapping of the two Rounds, and the
Night is drawing nigh when no man will be able to
work. When the Great Mother returns to the One
Eternal, she brings as it were the Sixth Race into unity
with Him, acting as a mediator between the two in a
sense. She is the Spirit that has mothered these people, and so when she returns into the One Spirit, this
relationship will continue and thus they will be united
with Him.

It is this which causes the bars to fall between the
upper and the under worlds; that is, the line of demarcation between Matter and Spirit. There is now no
sharp line between the two, but Buddhi is merged into
Atman, and from this time on there is nothing to check
the free passage from the one state into the other. In
fact they are now becoming but one world, in two com-
partments, and the way is open for the free passage
from one state into the other.

This will all be fulfilled in the year 1921, and so will
that indicated in the next Shloka, for that follows immediately upon the fulfillment of this one.

As to the farther work of this period, there is nothing
to be said, as it touches upon a mystery so Divine that
it would be improper to write it down, for it can only
be uttered at low breath from mouth to ear, let him
that readeth understand and farther this affiant saith
not. Face both East and West and in thy heart a Lily
and a Rose shall grow, and the Golden Light shall dawn
upon Thee, and when it does, look—behold—and be
Silent.

In the Sixth Shloka the Dragon of Wisdom is the
Buddh or Logos, the very essence of Kosmical Wisdom,
and the Dharma, the very essence of Kosmical under-

standing. We must, however, guard against the error of assuming that this is Divine Wisdom in the sense of the Divine Mysteries. The Dragon is always a symbol of Nature, the same as is the Serpent. It is the highest symbol of the Natural Wisdom and the Natural Mysteries, but is never used to symbolize the Divine Wisdom and the Divine Mysteries. The symbol of these is the Virgin Sophia, and hence at all times a woman. The Dragon of Wisdom is Kosmical Wisdom, that relating to the Manifested Logos. It relates to the Spirit as well as to Matter, but does not reveal Pari-Brahman. When this Dragon of Wisdom descends and incarnates in a man fully he becomes a Buddha, a fully Enlightened One, and when it incarnates in any man to the full extent of his Buddhi, he becomes a perfected Arhat. Its descending at this time means that the Buddhi of the Earth has become identical with the Kosmical Buddh, or the Logos, and hence is completely flooded by it. This means that the work of the Sixth Round is completed, and that the Sixth Race have completed their evolution, each one of them having become a perfected Arhat, and therefore on the threshold of Nirvana. At this time will come the Diamond Souled Host, that is to say the Nirvanic Vehicles or bodies. They are the perfected Spiritual Beings. Not new entities in the sense in which that term would ordinarily be understood, but rather the Sparks of Spirit, and the volume of Spiritual Energy and Substance which they insoul. When the Dragon of Wisdom has permeated the Kosmos, and thus caused it to finish its Sixth Round Evolution, these Spiritual Powers and Vehicles will descend and enter the realm of the Earth.

The forms created for them are the perfected Arhats, those who have finished the Sixth Round Evolution, that will mean the humanity of this Round, with the exception of those who have failed in the Round. These Nirvanic Sparks will enter the Atmas of the people, and the Spiritual Substance will enfold the Buddhi and the Spiritual Energy will energize it, and the result will be a complete change in them, making of them Nirvanees, at least so far as their Spirits and Souls are concerned, though of course it will take some little time for the Nirvanic state to descend through their Manas, Kama, Prana, and their Gross Body. Yet this is what has taken place as a result of the descent of the Diamond Souled Host, the Race of Arhats have entered Nirvana.

From this time on these people are no longer Maya's Sons, for they now have the inner senses opened. They are able to hear the Voice of the Silence, and the Soundless Sound, and have awakened their Spiritual Understanding and as a result the illusion disappears, and they see Matter as it is, a mode of motion of Spirit, that and nothing else. Common sense has disappeared, Maya has vanished, and Naked Truth insofar as any Manifestation, even that of the Spiritual World, can be spoken of as Truth. The Third and lower aspect of Maya, that of the World Illusion, is annihilated and they are brought into the Second phase. But as this second phase, that of the skipping and playing of Ishvara, is of comparatively little harm, they may be spoken of as free from Maya, because the Maya indicated in the Stanzas is the World Illusion. This has ceased for them and so they are now living in the Spiritual World. And this is while they still retain their Terrestial Bodies.

They are Sons of Will because they are free from all outside dominance, and are the products of their own Will. They are the Self perfected and Self evolved Ones, hence Sons of their own Will, the will to become Spiritual, that is the Spiritual and rising Will. They are Sons of Yoga, for Yoga is Union, no matter what path one has followed to reach it. They have accomplished the Union between their personality and their individuality, and as a result, the personality has been merged in the individuality and has therefore ceased to be. They are Free Souls, having attained complete emancipation from the bondage to the personality. All that pertained to the former state of illusion has vanished, and the humanity has freed itself and entered the realm of Light and Knowledge.

The time during which this is all to be realized will be the four years from 1921 to 1925.

When in the Seventh Shloka we are told that no more are the bars between the finite and the infinite to be raised, we are to understand that never more is there to be any line of demarcation between the Material and the Spiritual Worlds for they are to be one. Not only will this be the case with the humanity on the Earth, but also the Material Forces will be perfectly responsive to the motion of the Spiritual Forces and the one shall be lost in the other. There will in fact be no distinction between Matter and Spirit, for they shall act as two modes of the same thing, and there shall as a result be no longer any conflict between the two, but perfect harmony and unity shall reign supreme.

The reason for this will be that the Sixth shall fall into the Seventh with ease. The meaning of this is that the end of the Sixth Round has now come, and so it shall fall into, or be merged into the Seventh Round. The fact that this is to be with ease indicates that there will be no conflict of the elements at this time, and the time of Night will not amount to much, though of course it will cause some inconveniences. However, there will be no great disturbances such as have accompanied every other change from one Round to another. This will be due to the fact that the Sixth Round has been all the time, a period of preparation for the Seventh. It will also be due to the influence of those Seventh Race people who have been developed in the very beginning of the Sixth Round, being born and shaped by the Great Mother at that time. Their influence will hasten the time of the Seventh Round to which they in reality belong. It will also be greatly hastened by the influence of Kalki, for he comes to end the Kali Yuga, and to usher in the Sattva Yuga. Now bear in mind that he must end the Kali Yuga during his work as the Avatar, hence before he has laid aside the Sword the Kali influence must be at an end. Now at the termination of the Kali Yuga the Sattva Yuga must begin. It cannot be delayed at all, and the Sattva Yuga is the Seventh Round, hence the Seventh Round will have to commence during the life of the Avatar here on Earth. The change will also be greatly due to the presence on Earth of the Great Mother during the former part of the Sixth Round. She is Lakshmi, and as such, the great enemy of Kali. She comes to help Kalki to remove the Kali influence, and also to give birth to a new Kosmos. That which she bears and raises will be the Sattva Yuga, for Shri, the essence of Lakshmi, is the very Substance of Sattva. As a result of all these influences, it will be absolutely necessary that the Sixth Round should merge into the Seventh in a very few years. The greatest cause, however, for this merging, is the descent of the Diamond Souled Host, for they will make of all whom they enfold Nirvanees and hence Seventh Race people, and when the humanity has become inhabitants of the Seventh Round, of course, the Kosmos will have to respond, and hence it will be merged into the Seventh Round. We must not measure Spiritual things in Time, for on the Buddhic Plane there is neither Time nor Space, and when we come to the Nirvanic Plane this is doubly so. At this time the Kosmos will have become so much more plastic than it has been in the past, that it will not offer the resistance that it would have offered in any other age, and hence the transformation will go on at lightning speed.

The Sixth will be a very short Round, for it will only occupy the short period of forty-four years, from 1881 to 1925, at which time the last Shloka will have its complete fulfillment. The forces tending to finish this evolution will be at least ten thousand times as powerful as they have been at the time of any New Round in the past, and that is why in this instance the work will be accomplished in such a short time.

# THE STANZAS OF DZJN.

## THEOGENESIS.

### Stanza VIII.

1. At last the Full-toned Chord was struck by Maya's Sons, and at the sound Illusion vanished. Truth stood full revealed. Knowledge, Power, the glory of achievement clothed the newly born as a garment.

2. Adown the star-spangled path of the Gods—the path of lesser Lights awaiting birth in other forms—came One unlike the Gods, yet kin to them; like unto man, yet more than man; One clothed in raiment, glistening like the hoar frost in the sun; majestic, stern of countenance, yet soft of speech.

3. From lesser Light to Light He stepped, and as His footsteps pressed each Star it gave a chord of sweetest melody. As He drew near and nearer still, each new pressed chord was placed in song triumphant.

4. At length He halted, poised aloft and bent His ear to catch the song the Stars now sang so clear and strong from far beneath His feet.

5. The once Dark Star now shone with glory reflected from His face and full and clear He heard the echo of the chord which hitherto had sounded only minor tones of woe and anguish.

6. The King had come into His own and now was known to them. I am the first, He said, and I am last, and we are one. Out of the darkness hath come the light. Out of nothing hath come all things. Out of Death hath come Light eternal. It is done.

### COMMENTARY.

In the First Shloka the Full-toned Chord is the one which Fohat ordered to be struck in the Fourth Stanza. It could not be struck during the Fifth Round, for then only five notes sounded and the other two strings, those of Atma and Buddhi, jangled out of tune. It could not be struck during the Sixth Round, for then only six notes would sound, while the seventh or Atma would still jangle out of tune. Therefore the first time when it could be struck would be in the very beginning of the Seventh Round. The striking of this Full-toned Chord by Maya's Sons, means that all the Seven Principles acted in perfect Harmony, and at the same time responded in perfect Harmony with the same Full-toned Chord of the Kosmos, which was now completed also. That is to say, they were able now to respond to all the Harmonies of the Universe, which was now operating on all of its Seven Notes, and thus the Sevenfold Celestial Harmony was repeated in man. Their evolution was completed, and they were now awake in all of their Seven Principles. At this first sound Illusion vanished, for the reason that all Illusion is due to our inability to see things as they are, hence we get a mistaken impression of them. As long as we depend upon the Senses for our Ideas we will be deceived, for those Ideas are the results of our defective perceptions, and hence exist only in the mind. They have no Objective Existence, but are quite Subjective in their nature. It is this which makes the Illusion, for we have never seen any thing as it is, a Numenon, but only as it appears, a Phenomenon. This gives us an Ideal World which has no actual existence, and which the ignorant live in, and persist in calling the Real World. Even when one reaches the Buddhic Plane he is not free from the Illusion. It is true he is no longer deluded by this Ideal

World which held him in bondage while he was chained by the senses. He is now able to see things as they are, and thus realize the world of Kosmic Ideas, but still he has not reached the Ultimate. His Pure Reason can only deal with the Things which are given to it by the Pure Intuition, therefore it is dependent upon those things that are presented to it on the Buddhic Plane. He is living in an Actual World, which he takes for the Real World, but these things are but the acts of the Things in Themselves which are present in the Spiritual World or Nirvana. This is the Real World, the World of the Thing in Itself, the Monad. Until one is able to see and understand the Monad, he is still bound by the Illusion of Appearances and is unable to recognize the Reality. At the first Full-toned Chord, the Inner Senses were opened and man was able to see the Things in Themselves, the Monads, and through the Faculties of his Spirit to understand them. When he did this for the first time, the Illusion vanished completely, for he was able to see all things as they were in their ultimate essence, hence there was no Illusion for him any longer. The Four Lower Dimensions of Space vanished, and there were henceforth but Three, the Fifth, Sixth and Seventh, as they are now. The Square of Matter dissolved and the Triangle of Pure Essence alone remained.

Truth stood full revealed, for the reason that man was no longer deceived by the appearances, and was able to transcend the Relative, and to see all things in the Absolute. Henceforth there is and can be nothing concealed from him. Absolute Truth is his permanent possession. Being endowed with all ability to realize the Truth in the absolute, it was now possible for them at the same time to see it in its true relativity, that is as it is related to the source of things in the Spirit, and as it is manifested, hence the Knowledge of the Manifestation, as well as the Truth of the Unmanifest, was

alike their possession. Because of the unfoldment of
the Spirit, they had all the powers of the Spirit in a
state of liberty, so that they could use them as freely
as they now use their physical powers, that is to say,
they were as free on the Spiritual Plane as men are at
the present time on the Physical Plane.

The glory of achievement clothed them as a garment,
for now their Spiritual nature was set free, and they
were able to express all the latent qualities of their
Monad free from any limitation from the outside whatsoever. There was no limitation to their achievement,
within the range of the qualities of their Atma. Hence
they were clothed as with a garment by the Realities
of the Spiritual World, and no longer belonged to the
World Illusion. At this Fohat passed away and was no
more, for the Race had reached Human Perfection so
far as Type was concerned.

They are called the Newly Born for the reason that
they were now Seventh Race people and hence were assumed to have been born again. The Seventh Round is
Whirling, and the Seventh Race has appeared. This, of
course, does not mean that every individual has reached
this state at this time, but this is the characteristic Type
at that time and the stragglers are the exception and
not the general rule.

This will all take place in the early part of 1925,
when the Seventh Round must be in full swing.

In the Second Shloka the star-spangled path of the
Gods is the path of the diverse Kosmical Forces, for
that is all the Gods are; some of them are Spiritual
Forces, but the majority are Material Powers. It means
that the One descending was passing through these Powers and effecting them with His Spirit ere He reached
the Earth. He was passing through the region of the
Planets and the Stars ere he touched the earth. The
lesser Lights were those forces below man, that is, below the Spirit, and also below the level of those great
Powers. They were awaiting the time when Kosmical
Evolution would organize them into new forms suited
to the state of the Kosmos during the Seventh Round.

This One was unlike the Gods, or Kosmic Powers,
yet kin to them. That is, He was of a different order
to them. He was in fact quite Divine in the sense of
Para-Brahman, hence he was not like the Powers of

the Universe because He belonged to a much Higher
Octave. He was not even similar to the Spiritual Powers, for they are aspects of the Manifesting God, while
He is one with the Unmanifest God. In this way we
are able to see wherein He is unlike all of these Spiritual Powers. At the same time He is kin to them, for
the reason that they are all aspects of the Universal
Spirit, which is the First Emanation from the Divine
Spirit with which He is one.

He is unlike the Spirits of the Throne. Who are
they? The Throne is the seat of Para-Brahman the
Divine Spirit, and these Spirits are the Seven Spirits
of God, or the Seven Divine Principles, which are the
Archtypes of the Seven Principles in Nature and in
man. See the statement about them in Revelation.
These Seven Spirits of the Throne are not aspects of
Vishnu the Supreme, for He is the First Emanation
growing out of their activity. They are not the Good
Law, for this is the Fiat of their united Will. They
are the Seven Spiritual Sources of all Manifestations,
and ever abide in the very depth of Para-Brahman,
for they are the Seven Rays going to make up the
Pure White Light of Para-Brahman. He is unlike
these Spirits, because each one of them is only a single
Ray of the Seven Rayed Spirit, while the full Light
of Para-Brahman is completed in Himself. Yet He
is known of them, for the reason that He is their
Master. It is He that directs them, for it is through
Him that they, aye even the fullness of Para-Brahman
is able to shine forth to man and the universe. He
is the connecting link between the Absolute IHVH, the
Unnameable, the Word of Fear, the Eternal and Para-
Brahman which is His Essence, but of which He is the
Esse. Para-Brahman is the Essence of IHVH, but
this One is the very Esse of the IHVH. Thus He is
known and obeyed of the very Spirits of the Throne,
the Seven Spirits of God, or the Seven Divine Rays
of the Great White Light of Absolute Divinity, for
he stands between them and the Absolute IHVH Himself.

He is like unto man because He has been a man,
and retains the human memory and consciousness. At
the same time He is more than man, for he is a man
Apotheosized into the Ultimate Godhead, hence He is

the Perfected God, yet retaining the Form of a man, but with the Substance of His body quite Divine. That is, each of His Seven Principles is composed of one of the Seven Spirits of the Throne, in the place of one of the Seven Principles of Nature as is that of a man.

He is clothed in this glistening garment, for the reason that He comes clothed in His Divine Glory and not in a veil. It is the Radiance of the Divine Spirit, the Glory of God shining round about. He is majestic, for he is the very crystallization of the majesty of the Heaven of Heavens. He is stern of countenance, because He is the very Epitome of Divine Justice, and cannot look upon sin with the least degree of allowance. At the same time He is soft of Speech, for He is equally the Epitome of Divine Love, and thus is filled with Infinite Love and Tenderness for all that lives, has lived or ever shall live in the future. He is, in fact, the very Esse of the Ultimate God.

Who is this Divine One? He is One who, being in the Form of God, meditated no usurpation to be equal with God, but emptied Himself of his Spiritual Nature and became human, taking on the form of one of the servants, and therefore God has highly exalted Him far above Angel, and Principalities, and Powers, and given Him a name which is above every name, that at His name every knee should bow and every tongue confess of things in Heaven and of things in Earth, for by His own Name Jehova, which is IHVH has He called Him, and that is the Name that was given Him. He is now equal with the Father.

This is Jesus Christ in his Divine Glory as God the Son, and this is a description of His Second Coming for the purpose of His Messianic Reign upon the Earth, during the Seventh Round. It is the greatest possible mistake to confound Him with Kalki the Tenth and last Avatar of Vishnu, for Kalki comes to accomplish the work of the Sixth Round and to usher in the Seventh, and thus to prepare the way for the coming of Christ. He is in this sense the Forerunner of the Second Advent to the Gentile world, just as Elijah will return as the Forerunner of this Advent to the Jews. There is nothing which would fill Kalki with such horror as for any one to identify him with Christ. Even at the time of his first coming Jesus was not an Avatar of Vishnu, but of Para-Brahman, and before the time of His death he was the incarnation of the perfect Divine Nature, save in the case of constitution; that is, He was the Perfected Christos.

Why does He come to this Earth at all? He comes to Rule it, that it may pass to an even greater state, and that under His Divine Guidance all may pass into the state of Para-Nirvana, and ultimately into that of Maha-Para-Nirvana, and still continue to live upon the Earth, which will, under His guidance and fostering care, be so transformed that it will be fitted for such a Race of Beings to dwell upon it.

The time of this descent will be the same as that of the First Shloka; that is, the beginning of the Seventh Round, in the year 1925. Of this you can rest assured.

In the Third Shloka the lesser Lights are the minor Powers of the Spirit, and also some of the Powers just below it. They are not strong enough to be called Gods, but still they are Lights. His stepping from one of these to another, means that His influence has not only acted upon the Gods, the great Spiritual Powers, but it has now reached the lesser Spiritual Forces, or Lights, hence He is Spiritualizing all things, first in the Universal, and then in the particular. It also means the passing of this Divine Influence from one of the Heavenly Bodies to another, and thus their Spiritual Regeneration. His footstep pressing each Star means that each Star in the Heavens is to be gradually permeated by His Spirit, and thus transformed in its nature. All the Heavenly Bodies are active, are in fact Living Souls. Their activity manifests in a continuous vibratory motion, not only within them, but also in the Aura which floats out from them. They are each Septenary in their nature, having the Seven Principles, the same as Nature and man. This Motion is not chaotic, but is perfectly harmonious, being dominated by its keynote, and thus forming a perfect chord of harmony. This will also manifest in sound, which may be heard by the one who is able to hear with the Kosmic Ear. The sum total of these chords constitutes the Music of the Spheres. When He presses each Star it gives forth a chord of sweetest melody. It is not only harmony now, but also melody, the soul of music, and it is the sweetest melody, for the reason that His Spirit entering the Star, it has its Spirit set free and hence that Spirit joins in the chord, thus completing the Music of that star. In a word, as He nears the Earth, He so awakens the entire Material Universe that each part of it thrills with Spiritual Life, and hence it is all elevated into Nirvana. It is the awakening of all things to the Nirvanic Rapture, so that it will be made ready for the work of the Seventh Round, and there will be no unperfected object in all nature.

His drawing near and nearer still, means the approach to the Earth itself. Up to this time He has been acting upon the Stars remote from the Earth, but now He approaches it, for the time has come for its complete Regeneration. Each new pressed chord was placed in song triumphant, that is to say, each Star in the past has uttered a perfect chord of its own, though they have been separate and distinct; but now, as He draws nearer to the Earth, they are all merged into one, thus producing a Perfect Symphony, which is not what the Music of the Spheres has been in the past, for that was Fifth Round Music, but this is now Seventh Round Music, and contains the Note of Celestial as well as Kosmical Harmony. It is now the song of triumph, which means that the Kosmos has completed its Nirvana, insofar as its Spirit is concerned, and this Nirvana is now ready to descend into the Lower Principles, until the entire Universe in its Gross Body is Wrapped in the Bliss of Nirvana. Hence we are to realize that His coming is not so much for the sake of the people as it is to awaken the Spiritual Principle in all Nature, and cause it to spring forth into life, for the Whole Creation is travailing in Pain together until now, waiting for the manifestation of the Sons of God, that it may be delivered out of bondage into the same liberty as the children of God. He comes to set the groaning Creation free from its bondage to matter, and bring it forth into the life of the Spirit. This is the principal reason for His coming to Earth, though of course it is also for the purpose of delivering the Earth from the scourge of Sin, and bringing it into Unity and Peace, and also for the purpose of guiding the evolution of man back to Maha-Para-Nir-vana, the state of Bliss Eternal.

In the Fourth Shloka His halting, being poised aloft and bending His ear to catch the song the Stars now sang, indicates that while still far above the conscious-ness of humanity, His progress is at an end, He has reached the Earth, and is listening to hear if all the Universe of Stars has entered the new Rapture. This is seen to be the case, for they have all joined into the one song of triumph which now swells out from the depths of the entire Kosmos. It rings out clear, for there is no discordant note, and strong, for all the power of the hosts of the Stellar Heavens has entered into it, and has swelled forth with all the strength in it. In a word, all the Heavenly Bodies have attained Nirvana, and have joined their voices in the Celestial Harmony of that state. They have each and all entered the Seventh Round and are in full swing, and the Uni-verse as a whole is on the homeward sweep to the still more exalted state of the Spirit. The Earth alone holds them back, for He has not as yet touched it and thus quickened it into the fullness of Spiritual Life, so that it may enter into this song of triumph and thus enter into its own for the final struggle up to Para-Nirvana, and the Blessed state of Bliss beyond.

The Fifth Shloka begins with the time when He touches the Earth. It is at this time that the Regen-erating Influence which radiates from Him begins to energize the Earth itself. The Once Dark Star is the Earth. We learned in the Seventh Stanza that the Once Dark Star was changed, and shone with brilliant Light, but that was the Light that came to it during the Sixth Round, in comparison to what it is to be-come during the Seventh Round, it is still Dark, for it has not awakened to the Nirvanic State as yet. It now shines with the glory reflected from His face; that is, the radiance of the Divine Spirit which ever flows forth and shines forth from Him reflected itself upon the Earth, and it was transformed by the vibration set up by that reflection, so that it awakened the Spiritual Principle of the Earth, and this, respond-ing to that vibratory urge, swelled forth into the chord of Sevenfold Harmony. The Earth Spirit has awak-ened, and has come into His own, having broken the bonds of silence, which Matter has forged for Him, and so the full-toned Chord of harmony swells forth into union with the Sons of the Universe.) Full and clear is the echo of the chord which hitherto had sounded only minor tones of woe and anguish. This chord is the chord of the Earth. During the time when it has been bound by matter, it has of course been in the same miserable plight as the humanity that has inhabited it all this time. There has of course been nothing but woe and anguish, and hence the Earth Chord has sounded forth only those minor notes. The Major Note of Bliss can only be sounded by the Spirit, and all this time it has been stilled, but now at last it is loosed and the radiance from the Messiah has awakened it to action. It sounds forth the great Major Note of Joy and victory, and this swells out into the full Major Chord of the Spiritualized Earth. This now sounds full for all the vibrations of the Earth are brought into that Chord of Triumph, and hence all the Forces of Earth are proclaiming that sweet Harmony. It rings out clear, for there is nothing to mar its beauty now. It rings out full and clear, and its echo is heard in the Kosmos, and there unites with the song of triumph raised by the entire Universe. It has now joined the Great Spiritual Symphony, and so the Earth Chord is swallowed up in that Universal song triumphant, and they are one. The Earth has entered on the Seventh Round, and onward she swings until she has finished the return sweep to the Ultimate state of the Spirit. At first it may seem that this was realized in the Seventh Stanza, but this would be a mistake. What is there shown is that the Humanity of the Earth were born into the Seventh Race, and in the First Shloka of this Eighth Stanza we are shown the consummation of this for the Race. They are at that time in the Seventh Round, but it has not reached the Universe or the Earth as yet. Then comes the Divine One in the Second Shloka, and in the Third and Fourth Shlokas He has brought the Universe into that Round, but the Earth has not as yet entered it. In the Fifth Shloka it is shown how the Earth joins the Song Triumphant and enters the Seventh Round also. Now all is Nirvana, there is nothing below.

We must caution you against the idea that this work is to require any great length of time, for this would be a mistake. As He Leaves His Father's Throne of Glory He Enters the Star-Spangled Path of the Gods, and as He approaches the Earth, coming several million times more rapid than a Ray of Light, he passes from one Star to another, Regenerating them and in this way causing their Chord to sound forth true and sweet. At last as He hovers over the Earth, He causes all those Chords to blend into the Song Triumphant, and in this way brings the Universe into the full swing of the Seventh Round. ) Now, as this depends not on any development within the Universe itself, but is the instant result of the action of this Divine Radiance upon its Spirit, it will take place as soon as that Radiance has been reflected through and through the entire Universe, which will be in a very short time. At last' He rests upon the Earth, and the instant that He does its Spirit is thrilled with the New Life, and so it swings into the Seventh Round. All that is stated in this Fifth Shloka takes place in an instant of time; that is, the instant he stands upon the Earth.

This will all be fulfilled in 1925, for that is the time when He comes and this Shloka deals with the placing of His feet upon the Earth. From that time on we have the working of the Seventh Round and its Seventh Race; that is, the Race of Nirvanees.

The Sixth Shloka deals with the Reign of Christ on Earth. The first sentence covers a period of several thousand years, for it is practically the entire length of the Seventh Round. This reign will be a time of discipline for humanity, for He comes to rule over the nations with a Rod of Iron and to dash them to shivers and make them over again. You ask what will be the need of punishing a Race of Nirvanees? In the sense of the Divine Mysteries, Nirvanees may be as great sinners as the most material of people. There are in fact two kinds of sin—the first is that which grows out of the attachment to the objects of sense, and which will of course be a thing of the past with the Seventh Race. There is, however, another kind of sin—the sin which has its root in an individual will. It is this sin which came first, for it was that which caused the fall of man, and thus brought him into bondage to the senses and to matter. So long as man has an Individual Will in opposition to the Will of God he will continue to be a sinner in the Sight of God, and to need salvation. Now a Race of Nirvanees will have a more highly developed individuality, and hence a more powerfully individualized will, than any one on a lower level, hence they will be more disobedient to God than ever before. And this will not be so excusable as it has been before, for they will have more knowledge, and will be rebelling against more Light. When the King comes into His own, he begins this reign of chastisements, using His Divine Power as a means of enforcing His Will, and at the same time making use of highly perfected human beings, as His agents for the government of the Race, and their discipline by temporal punishments. In fact this is the purpose of the Para-Nirvanees and of the Maha-Para-Nirvanees who are now being developed. There has never been any period in the world's history before when these have appeared, but they are now being developed so that they may act as the Elder Brothers of the Seventh Race, just as the Nirvanees at the present time are acting as the Elder Brothers of the Sixth Race, and as the Arhats have acted as the Elder Brothers of the Fifth Race. His being known of them, relates to a period a thousand years later, when the Race will have accepted Him, and having obeyed Him absolutely, will have fixed their wills in that of God, and thus having cast off all Individuality will have passed to Para-Nirvana, and at last into Maha-Para-Nirvana.

He was the first because He was the Creative Logos that was with the Father, and by and through whom all things were produced. He is the last because this same Logos incarnated in the Human and became man, and later attained to the Perfection of the Godhead, and He was the First to realize this state. He then came to humanity again, and is the last one to resign all things to the Father. He is the final Perfection of all things, and during all this He has retained His identity. But above all things, in Him has been performed the entire Circle of Existence, for He was with the Father as the Logos, when there was nothing else. He was the point from which Emanation started. He

descended into the Human Nature, the descent of the
Spirit into Matter, and then went into death, from
which He began the ascent into Divinity, which He
realized in its fullness, being made one with the Godhead, which is the ultimate end of the highest evolution. Hence the Circuit of the Line of Life was completed in Him, and he is the beginning of Emanation
and the End of Immination, both in one. As a result of this He is King of the Cycle of Life, and Master of the whole design. Hence He is able to bring
Humanity into the place from whence they departed
when they began their descent into matter. And He
is One with the Race, for He is the epitome of all
Life and Evolution. What He has accomplished is the
way of the Great Return, and all who go that way
must abide in Him. He is the Self of all the Redeemed. Absolute Unity has been accomplished between God and Man and the Holy One; they are all
but One, and that is God, in the last analysis.

The Darkness here spoken of is the Darkness of
Matter. Out of this has been Evolved the Light of
the Spiritual state. The Law of Balance is perfect.
The Descent of the Universe into Matter has been the
means of the return into Spirit, and to a higher and
more perfect state of Spiritual Consciousness than
would have been possible if there had never been the
Descent into Matter. Spirit Descended into Matter,
and as a result Matter has Ascended into Spirit. The
Word was made Flesh, and hence the Flesh is made
the Word, it is the utterance of God. This has been
the natural result of the Eternal Law of Kosmic Evolution, which falters not, but works out all things to
their Logical End, be that what it may. And as it
never varies, but works on without variableness or
shadow of turning, its work is at all times perfect,
for it is the Divine Fiat working out into Life.

Things are but the Forms which the Infinite No-
Thing has assumed by reason of the Motion which was
imparted to it by the brooding of the Divine Idea;
hence this Divine Idea has caused this No-Thing, or
Formless Spirit to assume those Diverse Forms, which
are the Archtypes of all Things. Thus all things have
come forth from nothing, by the decree of the Fiat.

Out of the disappointments of sin and death, out of the misery and pain, and all the mistakes of life, has been developed the forces which have sprung forth into Life and Light Eternal. Not only this, but those Monads that have failed in the past will be reorganized and brought forth into Life once More, and will be brought to perfection. There are now none lost, but all have found the way of return, the dead as well as the living. This is at a period long after the end of the first thousand years, for thousands and thousands of years have passed. But while these people have overcome death they have at the same time overcome life. All selfhood is at an end. To them there is nothing but God and His Light, which is a mode of Himself. They neither live nor die, for life and death alike have ceased. They abide in the depths of the Light Eternal, which is the Glory of God or His Radiance.

It is done. The work of Evolution is at an end. The Seventh Round is at an end, and so has ended the Night following it. All rounds are over, and the Universe has ceased to move, for it is now at the Center, the point where all vibration ceases. It has been swallowed up in the infinite ocean of Divine Light, and has touched the center of the Fire of God. It is wrapped into the Shekina. All is over. Matter has returned to Spirit, and is Spirit; the soul has returned to God, and is God. The Great Return has been swallowed up in the source of all existence, and yet all things are. Nothing has ceased to be. But Thing and No-Thing are identical, and yet co-existent. The Apotheosis is complete. Aum! The Dewdrop falls into the Shining Sea! and it becomes the Shining Sea.

How were these Stanzas written? From whence was their source? How came man by such knowledge? Are they not a draft drawn from Revelation? No, my children, for these Stanzas were written thousands of years before the time of Christ. These last Stanzas are clearly a continuance of the same ones that are given in the Secrete Doctrine, and this one is simply the sequel to those which have been interpreted all the way along before. They all had to be written by the same person, for they are the same, and this last Shloka is but the Dramatical Climax of the entire series, and they must all have been written by the same hand. How, then, is it that the terminology is so identical with that of the Revelation? How better could one describe these great truths than by using this very terminology? This could not have been taken from Revelation for the reason that this Stanza teaches the Inner meaning of Revelation, and the Mystery of the Godhead, as well as the entire Mystery of the Christos and there are not five people in all the world who know this, and not one of them has ever seen this Stanza until after it was published in the Arti-zan. Whence, then, came the knowledge? Christian Mysticism is a revelation of the Ancient Divine Mysteries that were known in the dawn of human existence, and hence it teaches those things which were known in the ancient days, but have since been forgotten even by the Highest Adepts of the Great White Brotherhood. The Stanzas were written before the White Brotherhood lost the Key of the Divine Mysteries. But there is another item to be borne in mind. As all things that are transpiring or have ever transpired in the Kosmos are written in the Akashic Records, so is every Idea that has ever emanated from the consciousness of God, recorded in the Book of God's Remembrance, and there abides, and may be read by the one able to rise to the Plane where he can see it. These Stanzas were written by one who knew at first hand the Divine Design of Evolution. They are a treasure of Pre-Vedic Buddhism,. and therefore came direct from the Spiritual Consciousness of the Second Buddha himself. They are the Mind of God the All-Father, made known to us. He that hath an ear to hear let him hear this message from the All Divine in this time of trial, when we are so much in need of a Guide to point the way for us in the time of testing, during this Sixth Round, that we may fall into the Seventh and not fail in the passing.

Let every one who may chance to read this enter the closet in the center of his own Spirit, and there be still, and know that IHVH is God the One. And then let him breathe forth all the Essence of his soul in one Affirmation, "For all that Lives I live."

"Peace be unto all Beings."

## THE STANZAS OF DZJN.
## THEOGENESIS.
### Stanza IX.

1. From the East, the West, the North, the South come the four Holy Ones. On their way they gather the hosts of destroyers thronging their path, and set them in swifter motion.

2. At the ring "Pass Not" they pause, and with one accord cry unto Kwan Yin, "Speak thou but one word, a word of two parts, and we will bear that word "within the veil" upon our wings.

3. Then with a loud voice Kwan Yin gave utterance to the word. It shook the heavens and reopened the path between the fiery red star and the star which had been cleansed of its blackness.

4. Said he to the Holy Ones, "Gather your hosts and make fit habitation for the Angels of the Voice. They shall lead the new born Sons of Will and Yoga within the path I have opened, that they may people the fiery red star with a new race.

Daugma shall open their eyes to the glory of the hidden way.

#### COMMENTARY.

It is in the Fourth Shloka that the key is given with reference to the time of this Stanza. The Angels of the Voice are to lead the New born Sons of Will and Yoga within the path that is opened for them. Now it is only in the end of the Seventh Stanza, that is, when the Diamond Souled Host has been incarnated in the Sixth Race. Humanity that Maya's Sons become Sons of Will and Yoga, therefore it is the Seventh Race that is here alluded to, hence this Stanza relates to the Seventh Round, and therefore follows the Sixth Stanza, and is to a certain extent contemporary with the Eighth Stanza, describing another aspect of the work of the Seventh Round. The Eighth Stanza is concerned mostly with the Second coming of Christ, while this Stanza is concerned mostly with the Kosmical Regeneration that is to transpire through the activity of the Kosmical forces at the same time.

The East, West, North and South are the four aspects of the Universe. That is, they represent the Swastika in its Kosmical aspect, and stand for the positive and the negative poles of the Electrical and Magnetic Forces of the Kosmical Energies and all the Manifestations that flow from them during all time and space. The Four Holy Ones are those same Powers; that is, the positive and negative poles of the Electrical and Magnetic Forces in their Kosmic Essence. They are the Swastika of creation and destruction, which manifests in the Universe. The East, the West, the North and the South being the square of manifestation, while the Four Holy Ones are the Powers that manifest there. The coming of the Four Holy Ones means the awakening of these four powers and their concerted action to bring about a definite result. It means that the powers that manifest in creation and destruction are now being concentrated unto the end that a great change may be wrought in the Manifested Universe, which is in reality their manifestation.

The host of destroyers are all the centrifugal forces of the Universe, which are in the path of the Fourfold Force. These are all gathered up and concentrated on the work in hand, and as they respond to this force which directs them to the common point, they are set in swifter motion, so that their Destructive Force is accentuated far beyond anything that it has ever been in the past. This indicates that the work which they are to perform at this time is one of destruction; for the work at this time is the destruction of the present Earth that a new Earth may be born in its place.

In the Second Shloka, the ring "Pass Not" is the limit of all possible individual progress. It is the limit of the Sacred Chord on the Lyre of the Soul. For one to pass that limit he must transcend the individuality, and become something more than man. To pass this limit, means the realization of Para-Nirvana. Furthermore, it is the limit of the manifested universe, and therefore to pass this ring means to transcend the Manifested Universe, and to enter the realm of the Unmanifest. It is a ring, or circle, for it is from the Circle of Unmanifested Activity, or rather the activity of the Unmanifest, that the Manifested Universe on all of its seven chords is emanated. The Four Holy Ones pause here, for they are part and parcel of the Manifested Universe, and therefore they cannot pass into the Unmanifest region of themselves. It is the ring "Pass Not" to them quite as much as it is to any of the diverse Manifestations which flow from their activity.

Kwan Yin is the most beloved of all the Chinese Deities, being the one who "Looks upon" and "Hears the cries." It is in a certain sense feminine, and is more of a Goddess than a God, though the name is Neutral rather than feminine. She is the Magna Mater, the embodiment of Mother Love, and is therefore the Mother Principle of the Universe. She is in this sense the same as Lakshmi the Divine Mother. At the same time we are to realize that she is not so much the Mother who gives Birth, as the Mothering Principle which cares for the children after they are born. She is in this respect something like Hera as the protector of Childhood. She is the incarnation, or rather the Fountain of Mother Love, which nourishes all that are born. She is that principle of Mother Love which hears all the cries of her children, and looks down upon them in love and tenderness, nursing them and shielding them from evil. She is, in a word, the Mothering influence of the Spirit. This being the case, she is to be looked upon as the Mother of the Universe, and also as the Mother of everything that has been manifested. She is, therefore, the Mother aspect of Amatabha. Now as Amatabha is both Father and Mother, the two being one, she is Amataba manifesting Mother Love, therefore she is not feminine but neuter, though all the attributes she manifests as Kwan Yin are maternal and hence feminine. She is the neutral, or double sexed Amatabha, manifesting the feminine and maternal characteristics, and particularly Mother Love. Being Amatabha, she is incarnate in Amatabha Buddha, who thus becomes the incarnation of Mother Love, and is conceived as a female Buddha. She is incarnate in every Amatabha Buddha, however, and hence she is in this respect the maternity of the Buddha, just as Kwan Yin in the Kosmic sense is the maternity of Amatabha.

Now, a word is a creative power, for it is the positive outflowing of the inward idea, being the idea made manifest. Kwan Yin is requested to speak one word, a word of two parts. The speaking of a word means the placing in operation of the generative and maternal virtue of Kwan Yin. The two parts of the word indicate that it is to be both the generative and the formative virtues that are to be placed in operation. That is to say, it is both the Father and the Mother aspect that is to be concentrated in that expulsive effort of the Divine Will. It is the full force of Amatabha pulsating under the impulse of Mother Love. This will mean the setting in motion of a new aspect of the molding force, or rather the operation of the Mother influence in a new field. Kwan Yin, who has in the past listened to the cries of the manifested universe, is now besought to speak forth and thus give birth to something entirely new. This request comes with one accord from the Four Holy Ones, and is therefore the cry of the manifested Universe, for an inward expression of itself in the realm of the Unmanifest. If she will speak the word, they will bear it "within the veil" upon their wings. In other words, the prayer is, that the Four Holy Ones, or the creative Swastika, may be permitted to pass within the veil, beyond the ring "Pass Not" and there pursue their creative operations. It is the next step in the ascent of matter into Spirit. The work so far as the manifested Universe is concerned is completed, and now they, by reason of the fact that they have completed the work on this side of the veil, beseech Kwan Yin to give expression to them on the other side, so that they may operate in their creative aspect there in the region of the Unmanifest. This will, of course, mean the generation and birth of Para-Nirvanic creatures, who will be the children of Kwan Yin, possessing her own nature. It will also mean the generation and birth of a world which will be the manifestation of the fullness of Kwan Yin, and not a mere emanation of her. It will be Para-Nirvana manifesting in the organic form of the Universe. Evolution having returned to the point from which it started, it must now turn inward, and thus reach a step higher than it ever was before, as the fruition of the experi-

ences through which it has passed. The apotheosis
of nature must grow out of all the vicissitudes through
which it has passed. The result of all this will be
the regeneration and rebirth of the Kosmos on the
Para-Nirvanic Plane. And all this must in the very
nature of things be the result of the maternity of
Kwan Yin turning inward on her own Plane instead
of continually flowing outwardly on the planes below
her own level.

In the Third Shloka, Kwan Yin gives utterance to
the word in a loud voice. This means that a great
deal of force is put into the manifestation of her
maternity in this inward direction. It is not in a mild
manner, but with the concentration of all the force
of her maternity that the transformation is brought
about, and the effect must correspond to the force directed to that end.

This shook the heavens, for the old formation of
the Kosmos was shaken and began to disintegrate
when the generative and formative influence of Kwan
Yin was directed unto the generation and ultimate birth
of the new Kosmos. The Star which had been cleansed
of its blackness, is the Earth during the Sixth Round,
or rather the Earth as it was perfected in the Sixth
Round, hence the product of the Sixth Round. The
fiery Red Star is the Earth that is to be realized as
a result of this Seventh Round. In the beginning,
the fiery Red Star was the potentiality of the Earth,
and was what the Earth would have become if evolution had progressed upward instead of downward as
it did. But the fact is that evolution was downward,
the Spirit descending into matter, and hence the face
of the Earth was blackened. During the descent into
matter the path to the fiery Red Sar was closed, and
it has been closed during the ascent of matter into
Spirit, and will so remain closed up to the time Kwan
Yin speaks the word, for the reason that all the generative activities of Amatabha are directed toward the
material. Now, however, when she sends her generative virility inward and upward to the realization of
the new Universe, the way is opened from the state
of the cleansed Earth of the Sixth Round to the perfected Earth of the future; that is, the Para-Nirvanic
world. This means that the process of evolution is

started, which is ultimately to transform the star which has been cleansed of its blackness into the Fiery Red Star. The forces are now in operation, and the transformation will be ultimately realized as a result of the new trend of evolutionary law. One other thing which it is well for us to bear in mind here is that red is the color of the physical octave, and hence the star becoming red indicates the rebirth of the physical Earth, and does not relate to transformation in the interior principles of the Earth. It indicates that the gross physical vehicle of the Earth is to be regenerated and born anew. The fiery appearance indicates the great increase of the fire principle so that it becomes the dominant factor in the structure and composition of the Earth itself. Let us see if we can realize the importance of such a change as this. Ever since the descent of the Spirit into matter began, the preponderant element in the structure of the Earth has been carbon. The result has been a poisoning of the atmosphere so that it was difficult for life to continue here, and therefore the span of life has greatly shortened. Besides, the vehicles of man and beast have been so made up of this immobile carbon that they have with difficulty yielded to the higher vibrations, and therefore man has manifested a low order of intelligence and feeling, and in fact life has been more a state of inertia than otherwise. The intense activity of some nations and individuals has been an effort on the part of nature to overcome this carboniferous state, and to lift the race above it, but owing to the gross structure of the soul this strenuosity has merely led to the disintegration of the vehicles rather than to its metamorphosis as a rule. The black and the brown races are the embodiments of the carboniferous state of the Earth in a much greater degree than the other Races, and that is the reason why they will disappear and give place to the higher types, for the carbon will disappear also in the course of time. Immobility in the inhabitants of the Earth is the outgrowth of immobility in the Earth itself. The life upon the Earth reflects the condition of the Earth itself, and as the cause of this immobility in the life upon it is the presence of a preponderant quantity of carbon in the Earth, it follows that the only cure for these troubles is by reducing the proportion of carbon in the composition of the Earth. It is this which causes the gross materialism of the people, and the world can never be converted until the percentage of carbon is reduced in the Earth. The problem then is the reduction of the percentage of Carbon in the composition of the Earth. There is but one way in which to get rid of carbon. It must be burned. To do this we must have an increase in the percentage of Oxygen or the Fire principle, and in this way the Fire vibration will destroy the carbon, and will reduce it to a minimum. This is what will take place, and as a result of the great activity of the Fire vibration the major portion of the carbon will be consumed, so that the Earth will predominate in oxygen or the Fire principle. This will remove the grossness and opacity of the physical vehicle of the Earth. Will render it more brilliant, transparent and aerial. It will greatly reduce its specific gravity, and will increase its electro-magnetic force. The result will be a new Earth, which will have little resemblance to the present one. In the past it has been necessary for nature to cause dense growths of vegetation to cover the Earth in order that the carbon might be taken up by them and in this way life might be possible, but in the new Earth the carbon will be consumed to a great extent, and therefore these dense growths of vegetation will die out, and there will be no more jungles and dense forests, but only beautiful groves of trees and arbors of vines. All this will be but the natural outgrowth of the disappearance of the carbon from the structure of the Earth except in a small percentage.

It is to this transformation through the activity of the Fire Principle that the Bible refers when we are told that the Earth is to be destroyed by Fire. It is not the Earth in the absolute that is to be destroyed, but rather the carbon is to be burned up, and as this constitutes the major portion of the composition of the Earth as it is at present, this will mean the destruction of the present Earth. At the same time the transformation from carbon to oxygen will be going on all the time, so that as the carbon disappears the oxygen will take its place, so that the Earth will be here all the time, and will be just as large at the finish as it was at the beginning, and yet it will not be the same Earth. Yet there will no part of it be gone. It will be a case of regeneration and rebirth, which has taken place so gradually that one will scarcely notice the change. At the same time it is to be borne in mind that the life will continue on the Earth during the entire transformation.

This consumption of the carbon in the composition of the Earth will cause a corresponding consumption of the carbon in the composition of the bodies and souls of all the creatures living on the Earth, including the humanity on it. It is this burning up of the superabundance of the carbon in them that is indicated in the torments with fire and brimstone which are depicted in Revelation. This will be of necessity a very painful process, and it is most vividly described in that book. The Golden hued Race will be the embodiment of this Fire principle, for Gold is the Fire metal. They will have bodies that will gradually become transparent as the carbon is burned out of them. This will lead to a much more active, vital and intelligent Race of people, for they will respond to the Fire Vibration and will therefore have the fiery mind, and the fludic bodies resulting therefrom. As a result there will be little or no waste, and man will live forever when the carbon has been burned out of his nature, and when the atmosphere is no longer poisoned with it. The Earth will in this way become fiery and shining, even emitting light at all times. When it is self luminous there will, of course, be no such thing as darkness. It is of this time and condition that Revelation alludes when the Holy City of New Jerusalem is described, and we are told that the glory of the Lord did lighten it; for the glory of the Lord and of the Divine Race will be reflected in the Fiery Earth. It is, of course, true that the source of this light will be the members of the Divine Race living at that time upon the Earth, but at the same time they could not manifest their presence here unless the Earth was fitted for their abode. This is a great mystery, and I dare not lift the veil farther, for the Holy Things are only to be given to the Holy, but enough has been stated to give the key to the children of the Light. Let him that hath ears to hear give heed to what has been revealed.

The reopening of the path to the Fiery Star means the concentrating of the Fire principle so that it may consume the carbon and thus bring into a realization this great transformation. That is, it is the beginning of this process of transformation, and the direction of Kosmical Evolution unto that end. And this is the effect of the generative influence which Kwan Yin brings to bear upon the Spiritual Universe and the material universe as well. This is what is meant by the Holy City descending down from God out of Heaven to the Earth, for the Earth is to be born of the Spirit. For only in this way can it be suited to the residence of a Spirit born humanity.

In the last Shloka Kwan Yin bids the Four Holy Ones gather their hosts, that is the host of destroyers, and make fit habitation for the Angels of the Voice. The Angels of the Voice are those who are born as a result of that Voice. When Kwan Yin spoke, the word, which as we have seen was the inward expansion of the generative and formative energy of Kwan Yin, began to organize forms which corresponded to the very nature of Kwan Yin, and which were therefore her children of her own nature, and subject to no individual limitation. They were people in whom the non-ego was realized in its fullness. This new Race of Para-Nirvanic humanity are the Angels of the Voice; that is, they are the messengers who are to make manifest that voice, or rather the energy which flows forth in that way. The Earth can only be made a fit habitation for these Para-Nirvanees by the destruction of the carboniferous element that renders all life gross. It is therefore that the host of destroyers, or the centrifugal forces are directed in their attack upon the carboniferous element in the Earth, and not only upon its physical aspect, but also upon its interior principles as well. In this way the elements that stood in the way of the Higher state are eliminated and the Earth is made a fit habitation for the Para-Nirvanees or Angels of the Voice. But at the same time that it is made a fit habitation for them it is rendered unsuited for the abiding place of a material race of people.

The New born Sons of Will and Yoga are the Seventh Race humanity that is perfected as the last act of the Sixth Round and the beginning of the Seventh Round. These will be led by the Para-Nirvanees or Angels of the Voice in the upward way,( in the path that has been opened. This means that under the guidance of the Angels of the Voice they will eliminate the carbon from their nature and will be brought into that state where the Fire principle is their dominant element not only in their bodies but in their interior principles as well. In a word, the Angels of the Voice will be the Elder Brothers of the Seventh Race humanity, and will in this way help them to incarnate all of the virtue of the Fiery Red Star. This path will, when followed to the end, bring the Seventh Race to that point where they will have completely embodied the fire principle and will have become suited to the work of peopling the Fiery Red Star. They will in this way become a New Race, the perfected Seventh, the Race of Fire Men, and will at the same time be perfectly spiritual. This is the New Race that is to people the Fiery Red Star, a Race partaking of its own nature, and being the individualizing in human life and consciousness of the very nature of that Star itself; that is, of the Fire principle on all of the planes of nature. Thus the bright Fiery and transparent Race will have come to the Earth or rather will have evolved here on the Earth. Ye will call to mind the promise of Daniel the prophet that they that be wise shall shine as the brightness of the firmament (the Sun). Well, this is the meaning of it, for they will be bright and glorious even in their bodies, for the Fire body will have so transformed the lower vehicles that they are but vehicles for its expression, and have become in a certain sense fire bodies also. We are therefore to realize that there are to be formed two Races during the Seventh Round—the Angels of the Voice, a Para-Nirvanic Race, who are to be the guides of evolution during the Round, and also the Seventh or Nirvanic Race, who will be led by them. At the same time it would appear that the ultimate end of the Seventh Race is to realize Para-Nirvana itself, so that they will all be born as children of the Voice, for only such will be suited as the Rulers and Masters of the Fiery Red Star. Thus will they come to realize all that their Teachers have realized before them, for this new Race with which the Fiery Red Star is to be peopled is not the Seventh Race, for the Sons of Will and Yoga are that race. The new race is the perfected race, which has transcended individuality and are the perfect children of Amatabha. They will be the children of Light and Fire, for when all things have been made new, and there is a new Earth, there will of necessity have to be a new race to people it, for, bear in mind, the new Earth is not the Earth of the Seventh Round, but the Earth that is to follow after it. There are Seven Rounds for the present Earth, and at the end of the Seventh Round we must enter a new cycle, when the Earth will slip beyond the ring "Pass Not," and will begin a new era, on the Para-Nirvanic Plane, for the Earth as well as the humanity upon it must be saved. It is impossible for the Race to be saved until the Earth is saved. It is this that is indicated by the drawing of the Universe into Vishnu. This indrawing of the Universe is merely its slipping within the ring "Pass Not," and thus entering its Para-Nirvanic cycle of life. The descriptions as given in the book of Revelation are admirably suited to this apotheosis of the Earth, but sadly out of place as descriptions of Heaven. Let all who have ears to hear, ponder upon those descriptions as given in Revelation, and compare them with this disclosure and they will see the mystery as it is, but there cannot be anything more stated here, for the mystery is for the children of Light, and farther, this affiant saith not.

The time at which the work of this Stanza will take place will be some time after the year 1925. That is to say, it will begin at that time or a little after, and the first two Shlokas refer to practically the same time, for they will cover but a moment as it were. The Third Shloka begins at that time also, for all these only cover a period of a few years from 1925 onward. However, this and the last Shloka cover a period of several thousand years, for they cover the entire period of the Seventh Round, and bring us to the time of the New Earth. It is not possible to give any more accurate dates than these, for the reason that these two Shlokas relate more to the evolutionary process than to any

definite event, and this process will cover an immense
period of time. It may be stated, however, that the
preparation of the habitation for the Angels of the
Voice will not have been completed for a thousand
years, for this is undoubtedly the work of the milleni-
um, and the work of leading the Sons of Will and
Yoga, while it will to some extent go on during this
period of time, will have its real time of operation
during the ages that follow after the first thousand
years. Beyond these rather meager details there is
nothing that can be stated with reference to the time
of the diverse operations. At least it has not been
given at the present time. In case the time is indicated later on, and it is best to give it out to the public, the dates will be furnished.

For further light on this subject, as well as upon
the entire mystery of the new Earth and the new
Heavens, the student is advised to read very carefully
the last few chapters of Revelation, and take the matter into the Silence quite frequently, and it is possible
that as a result he will experience a measure of initiation. But that which has not been stated here can not
be given out, save at the door of the Sanctuary, and
at the foot of the Altar. He that hath ears to hear,
let him hear.

Daugma is a purified soul, a great initiate or the
Central Spiritual Sun, according to the way it is used.
The primary meaning, however, is the Central Spiritual
Sun. It becomes a purified soul or a great initiate
for the reason that they are so many incarnations of
the Central Spiritual Sun with a greater or less degree of perfection. Now, inasmuch as the New born
Sons of Will and Yoga are all purified souls, and great
initiates, for the reason that they have all attained
Nirvana, and hence are the very highest initiates even
before they have started on this new path, Daugma,
who is to open their eyes, can be neither, and hence
can only be the Central Spiritual Sun. Not only is
this true, but it is this New Race of Sons of the Fire
that are to have their eyes opened. The Central Spiritual Sun is the same as Vishnu the Supreme or Amatabha, though it is more Vishnu, for it represents the
masculine side more than the feminine side. Water
being the feminine principle, the Moon would represent

the Lakshmi principle, just as breath and fire are the masculine principle, that is Vishnu. This is the same as the Radiant one and the One Eternal in some of the earlier Stanzas. He is to open the eyes of the New Race on the Fiery Red Star to the Glory of the Hidden Way. Glory is the brightness, the outshining and the manifestation, therefore they are to behold the manifestations of the hidden way, so that they will be able to tread therein. The hidden way is the way that has been hidden for all time in the past, and which no one has been able to enter. It is the transcending of the ring "Pass Not" and the full and complete entrance into that higher state which will lead them up to the day "Be with us." In a word, it means the perfected evolution of Para-Nirvana. This means that the New Born Race are to see the way that will lead them to Para-Nirvana, and walking therein they will in turn become the same as the Angels of the Voice, though they will not be Angels of the Voice, for the reason that the Angels are the messengers of the Voice, and when the entire humanity has reached that state there will be no one for them to bear the message to, for all humanity will be walking in the Hidden Way. They will more properly be the children of the Voice.

Now, when this state has been reached, and all humanity has been brought into the glory of the hidden way, so that there is no one who has not accomplished the impossible feat of passing the ring "Pass Not," the Earth itself as well as the entire Universe will respond to the same condition, and thus the square of matter will fall into the triangle of Spirit. The four lower dimensions of space will disappear, as the four lower principles are drawn up into the three higher. Matter will have been apotheosized into Spirit as it were, and all the lower principles will have been merged into Atma-Buddhi-Manas, which will be the triangle of life during the time that is to come after this. This will be the case both with the Earth and with the life which is upon it. In other words, all things will have been elevated to Para-Nirvana. It is in this sense that all things are to be indrawn by Vishnu, the Central Spiritual Sun. This does not mean the disappearance of form, but rather the Spirit-

ualizing of all forms, so that they will represent the
Mind state and not that which is below. Thus we
have the disappearance of the Heavens and the Earth
that was during the Seventh Round and a New Heaven
and a New Earth that is to come as a result of the
reign of Christ on Earth. Daugma opening their
eyes, means that the presence of the Central Spiritual
Sun within the soul of each one will enlighten his
understanding, so that he will see all things as they
are in the consciousness of the Central Spiritual Sun.
Therefore is it stated that Daugma opens their eyes
to the glory of the hidden way, for this hidden way
is the way of expressing the nature of the Central
Spiritual Sun in individual life in a certain sense,
though in the absolute there is no individual in this
state of being. It will at the same time mean the
expression of the very nature of the Central Spiritual
Sun in the organic Universe. It is in fact the organization of the entire Universe upon the plane of
the Central Spiritual Sun, and the manifestation of
that which in all past ages has been unmanifest. In
the beginning the Spirit descended into matter, and
from the time of the beginning of the Sixth Round
matter ascends into Spirit, but there is this difference,
that whereas it was essential that Spirit should descend into matter in order that forms might be organized, in the ascent of matter into Spirit, these
forms will not be lost, but will merely be transmuted
as to their Materia, so that they shall become Spirit,
and will express not individuality, but the fullness of
the Central Spiritual Sun. Therefore the material
Universe will have reached a point higher than the
manifested Universe ever was before. This means that
we are not simply to cover the ground we have passed;
that is, to get back to the same point from whence
we descended, but rather that we are to gain experience through this circuit that will elevate us higher

than we ever were, or ever could have been, without such a descent and ascent. We are therefore to begin an entirely new cycle of existence, not below the plane of the Central Spiritual Sun, that is as to our Spirits, but upon its own level, though of course we will continue to function on the Buddhic and Mental planes. The Red and the green octave will disappear, and the Universe will manifest only on the blue, orange and yellow, and it will also manifest the indigo octave in its activities. Thus will the Central Sun itself be manifested in organic form.

# THEOGENESIS

———

## PART TWO

———

## The Foundation of Hermetic Philosophy

## HERMETIC PHILOSOPHY.

Thoth-Hermes is Kosmic Thought. Now we must differentiate between this Kosmic Thought and thought in the ordinary sense of the term. When man at this time uses the word thought, he has in mind that mental action which grows out of a sensation, that Intellectual Apprehension that follows a perception through the senses; or else, that Comprehension which grows up in the mind as a result of some previous Apprehension which survives in the memory, or the mental faculty, resulting in a spontaneous act of mentation. In either case the thought is the result of sensuous contact with an object in the sensible world. According to the Nominalists, all thought is of this nature, that is, mind generated through the act of contact with the Sensible World. However, the Realists hold another view. According to them there is a realm of Thought above the region of the Sensible World. This is the realm of Ideas of Plato, and of the Logoi of the Stoics. It is the realm of Kosmic Thought which is above all sensible Objects. It is, in a word, the Super-Sensible or Intelligible World. To understand this proposition, one must assume a Kosmic Mind, a sort of Impersonal Thinker, that is continually thinking Kosmic Thoughts, a process of Kosmic Ideation. This will give us the Logos of the Gnostics in its lowest aspect. It is this Kosmic Reason, that is not a person, but a Universal principle of Rational Activity. This Kosmic Reason, by reason of its very activity, is originating Kosmic Thoughts, and at any moment of time, the sum total of those thoughts will constitute the Intelligible World at that particular time. Thus we have a state of Kosmic Ideation precedent to the existence of the Sensible World. These Kosmic Thoughts are the causes of all those modes of activity which constitute the Things as they are, or Noumena; therefore these Kosmic Thoughts have a Real existence, whereas the sense engendered thoughts have only a nominal existence. To understand the problem, one must grasp the doctrine of the Indivisibility of Duration. This means the total repudiation of Mechanical Uniformitarianism. This latter view holds that the Universe is a Mechanism that moves as it is acted upon by a Force that directs it, and hence Duration is but a series of mechanical actions that eventuate in certain things that are to be apprehended through the senses and the Mind acting under the stimulus of those senses. From the former point of view the exact reverse is the case. The Universe is alive. Duration is the activity of a living principle that is ever acting upon Substance and in this way transforming it into an ever progressive sequence of new modes of life. This makes of the Universe a self-evolving Substance permeated by a self-evolving Life. From this concept we come naturally to that of Self-Consciousness as the first result of self-evolving Substance. Self-Consciousness being the essential characteristic of Living Substance, we must conceive of a Mind or Reason as the essence of this Living Universal Principle, an Abstract Thinking Substratum anterior to all things. This Kosmic Thinking Principle must, in the very nature of its being, generate Thought. Every such thought will be the Spiritual Word anterior to all that may spring forth from it. These Spiritual Words are the Logoi which are the realities back of the Sensible World. Thus we have the Living Process of Ideation engendering the Pure Ideas of the Ideal World. These are the Platonic Ideas. These Ideas acting upon the Plastic Substance or Materia, engender the Noumena, which are the things in their reality. The Sensible World is in reality the Subjective Picture that is presented to the Consciousness of the individual by the senses, and hence it is purely phenomenal, consisting not of realities, but of appearances.

Thoth-Hermes is the name given to the Living Process of Kosmic Ideation above outlined. He is at once the Scribe and the Instructor of the gods. This is only understood when we realize that there are two orders of gods. These we will call Kosmic and the Super-Kosmic gods. The Super-Kosmic gods are the Forces of the Pure Spiritual Realm, abiding back of the Manifest Universe. It is their activity that engenders this Sub-stratum of Kosmic Ideation. For this reason it is the expression as Living Consciousness of their activity. This Kosmic Ideation becomes the Scribe of the Super-Kosmic gods for the reason that all of its Thoughts are the Words engendering the Things of the Manifest Universe. This manifestation of the Super-Kosmic gods in the form of living forces that are ever evolving into Universal Form is the writing down of the Divine Words of the Super-Kosmic gods in the form of the Spiritual Words of the Principle of Kosmic Ideation. He is also the Instructor of the Kosmic gods, for the reason that they are but the Modes of Evolving Life growing out of the Kosmic Ideation. They are the Evolutionary processes that are engendered by Kosmic Thought, and therefore, the active manifestation of that very Principle. These forces of Creative Evolution, being the continual expressions of Kosmic Thought, are continually subject to its control, and are therefore said to be instructed by Thoth-Hermes. He is instructing them in the sense that the Writing or Spiritual Words of Hermes are to them spoken as the Intellectual Words, which therefore become the Self-Consciousness of those Creative Evolutionary Processes, or Kosmic gods, and therefore regulate their modes of activity. They are in this way made to act intelligently and not blindly. There is no such thing as a Blind Force in Nature. The Intellectual Words of the gods become the Living Words of the Forces of Nature, which have a determinate Destiny appointed to them in this way. The Living Words of the Forces of Nature cause them to act upon Matter in such a way as to impart to it the Vegetative Words which determine its growth, so as to order the development of the Universe in accordance with the Hermetic Writing. From this activity there is engendered in the Organized Universe the Sterile Words which have no power to introduce mutations in its form, but can only perpetuate that which has been established by the higher Forces of Creative Evolution. It is for this reason that there is no truth in the theory of Physical Evolution, Creative Evolution being the modes of the living manifestation of Kosmic Thought acting upon the Plastic Medium.

This being the nature of Thoth-Hermes, Hermetic, which is of the nature of Hermes, must in the very nature of things deal with the process of Kosmic Thought, that is, with Kosmic Thought as a Universal Principle, with the active process of Kosmic Thinking, and with the Kosmic Thoughts engendered by this thinking process. Hermetic Philosophy is the synthesis of those aspects of the Kosmic Mind into a Philosophical System. In a sense it is the Psychology of the Kosmic Mind. It must deal with Kosmic Thought both in its Essence as the Scribe of the Super-Kosmic gods, and in its Essence as the Instructor of the Kosmic gods. Hermetic Science is the relation of Kosmic Thought to all the processes of Creative Evolution worked out in detail so as to show the mode of evolving nature. Hermetic Art is the application of this knowledge of the mode of Creative Evolution to the practical work of controlling those very forces in a limited degree. Therefore its two principal departments are Magic and Alchemy.

The field of Hermetic Study is not the Sensible World but the Ideal World, therefore we do not follow the Inductive Method in any sense whatsoever. The Data accumulated through the activity of the senses is of no value. The beginning of our study is the Psychology of Thoth-Hermes. We must bring the Pure Reason and the Pure Intuition to bear upon the nature of the Sub-stratum of Kosmic Ideation, and must analyze the entire process of Kosmic Thought. After this, the relation of that Thought to the process of Creative Evolution must be traced out deductively. This will give to us the true understanding of the process of Evolving Life. This is what we might call the Hermetic Conception of the Universe.

The Hermetic Mysteries are the synthesized truth with reference to Kosmic Ideation, and the Creative Evolution which results therefrom, presented in such a manner as to veil the true meaning from all but the Initiate, and to reveal it to him. For this purpose, it is presented under the veil of Allegory and Symbol. Hermetic Initiation is two-fold. In the first place it consists in the unveiling of the Mysteries through interpretations so that the Mystae will be able to understand their meaning. This is done through the intellectualizing of the Mysteries. In the second place, it is through the gradual awakening of the latent faculties in the Mystae so that they are able to see the meaning of the Mysteries from within.

There are two classes of Initiates: The Mystae, who are learning the meaning of the Mysteries, and are in this way on the way to an understanding of the nature of Kosmic Thought, and the Epoptae who have reached the position where they are able to behold Kosmic Thought with the eyes of their understanding, and thus to read the writing of the Scribe of the gods. All previous training is to fit one for the task of reading the Writing, but the Epopt must read the writing, and in this way ascertain the nature of Creative Evolution and all the Mysteries of Nature at first hand. From this time forth he requires no Teacher, for the reason that he is able to read the writing, and therefore be taught by Hermes Himself. Such reading of the writing, which simply means the Intuitive Apprehension of Kosmic Thought in its pure Essence and of the diverse Kosmic Thoughts, is the meaning of being Initiated by Hermes. The Elder Brother is merely the Pedagogue who leads the Pupil to the School of Hermes.

When the Epopt has read the Writing of Hermes, that is, when he has acquired an understanding of the process of Kosmic Ideation, and likewise of the realm of Noumena engendering Thoughts, he must bring his Understanding to bear upon the Problem of Synthesizing the whole into an harmonious Unity.

When this work has been accomplished he will have mastered Hermetic Philosophy. Being now a Hermetic Philosopher, he must trace out the workings of the Forces of Creative Evolution, until he is able to grasp the entire process in a synthesized form, thus having a perfect comprehension of the entire realm of Hermetic Science. Having completed this work and thereby become the Master Hermetic Scientist he is ready to begin the study of Hermetic Art. To do this he must make use of the processes of Creative Evolution, which he now understands, in such a way as to accomplish practical results, in a word to carry on the work of Creative Evolution on his own account. To do this he must acquire the Hermetic Will, in a word embody the Living Word and make use of it in the control of the Forces of Nature and of Matter. When all departments of this operation have been mastered, and he has incarnated the Living Word and made it active unto the transformation of Matter he has mastered the Hermetic Art, and is, indeed, the true Hermetic Artist.

From the above it will be seen that Hermetic Philosophy is not a theory, or a School of Philosophy; it is a perfect Synthesis of Absolute Truth. It is the Mind of the Kosmos translated into terms of human understanding. The Consciousness of the Kosmos becoming a matter of Individual consciousness to the Hermetic Philosopher, he arrives at Kosmic Consciousness within himself. The teaching liberates man from the errors of Nominal and imparts to him Real Knowledge. It is, therefore, the Philosophy of Life of the Kosmos plus the incarnation of the Self-Consciousness of the Kosmos as a matter of Individual Evolution. The Epopt is therefore both a Mystic who has ensouled the Kosmic Self-Consciousness, and at the same time a Philosopher who understands the workings of Kosmic Thought as a problem that he has mastered. He is both the Thinking Subject and the Object of his thought.

## THE HERMETIC BROTHERHOOD.

A Brotherhood to be truly Hermetic must in the very nature of things be of the nature of Hermes, that is, of Kosmic Thought. In a word, it must be composed of men who are of the nature of aspirants for the realization of the Hermetic State. It is through such a Brotherhood alone that the Hermetic Mysteries can be presented to humanity. From the time the Hermetic Philosophy was first known, and the Hermetic Mysteries made known to men, there were Hermetic Brothers. As a man becomes possessed of an understanding of the Hermetic Mysteries, this knowledge exercises a transforming influence upon his consciousness and hence upon his character. The ordinary human consciousness is built up from the Apprehension of the Senses, and therefore it must in the nature of things be sensuous. It is this sensuous intuition that builds up the consciousness of the personality. When one has arrived at supersensuous knowledge his thinking must be of a different order to what it has been while all his ideas were drawn from the Apprehension of the Senses. This change in his thinking will reconstruct his Mind and Reason, so that he will not be the same as he was before. The man on the plane of sense perception and sensuous thought is but the individualization of his sense perceptions, and in like manner the man who is on the Plane of Supersensuous Thought is the Individualization of certain aspects of the Ideal World, to-wit, his Supersensuous thinking. As he attains unto a knowledge of the Thoughts of Thoth-Hermes, the thinking of those thoughts will transform his entire being until he becomes their image, and not only that but the form through which they manifest in consciousness. This will mean a complete transformation of the entire being so that he will not be the one he was before, but on the contrary be an entirely different personality. In this way he is born again, becoming the creature of Kosmic Thought, being born of Pure Kosmic Ideation. Thus are born the children of Thoth-Hermes. Their whole character is derived directly from Kosmic Thought. Heredity, environment and Planetary Influences have absolutely nothing to do with them. Not only this but all Karmic Influences fail, for they are born of the nature of Thoth-Hermes. These persons are but the crystallized expressions of Kosmic Ideation. Of course such an one will have to be an Epopt. There are others who are going through the transformation that is to result in such a birth, but have not been born as yet. Those Sons of Hermes are, by reason of the fact that they are born of Kosmic Thought, of the same nature, and hence brothers. The sum total of such Hermetic brethren constitute the Hermetic Brotherhood.

Thus it is to be seen that we have here, first of all, the Brotherhood of Epoptae, or sons of Hermes; and, second, a number of others who are on the way to that state. Children of Kosmic Ideation on the way to be born of that state. These are the ones who are being transformed from the human consciousness into the Images of Kosmic Thought. The Brotherhood will therefore contain two elements, those who are going through a period of change which is to result in their birth as Epoptae, and in the Epoptae who have been born of Kosmic Ideation. Thus it will constitute a sort of training school for the ensouling of Kosmic Ideation, together with those who have perfected the process. The different Degrees in the Brotherhood will indicate the stages at which one will arrive at different times while engaged in this process. That is to say, each Degree will represent a corresponding Degree of achievement in the realization of the goal. Initiation represents the actualization within the selfhood of the brother of a certain degree of Hermetic Wisdom. It is not sufficient for him to understand it from an objective standpoint, but he must actually become ensouled by that degree of the Truth. The realization of this state will constitute that particular Initiation. Neither is this all, but he must, through a gradual process of elevation of his consciousness, actually elevate himself above the diverse lower activities of the world as well as of the Individuality. There is also a process of polarization going on all the time, which will enable him to bring the diverse aspects of his selfhood into union with the diverse Words of the Hermetic Writing. In the Outer Court he must purify his body and then polarize it with the Sterile Word of the Universe, so that the two become one. In the First Degree his Astral Body must be purified so that it may be polarized with the Living Word of the gods, and the two may become one. In the Second Degree his Mind must be purified and then polarized with the Intellectual Word of the Hermetic Writing. In the Third Degree his Soul must be so purified that it may polarize with the Spiritual Word, Thoth-Hermes himself, and the two may become one. In the Fourth Degree his Spirit must be so purified that it may polarize with the divine Word of Phta, and with the Super-Kosmic gods themselves. This is the course of evolution which is reserved for the true Sons of Thoth-Hermes. We may speak of them as the Sons of Truth and Light, while those who individualize the impressions of sense are in reality the Sons of Illusion.

But we must bear in mind that the mere personnel of the Brotherhood is not its only strength. Every one is continually generating diverse fluids that may be generally classed as Magnetism, though the major portion of them are super-physical. These Magnetic Emanations, which are continually being thrown off by the ones who generate them, are at every moment being specialized by the vibration of the one who is generating them, so that every moment the fluids generated by him are the very Essence of his personality. These Magnetic Fluids are the exact fluidic correspondence of the men who generate them, therefore there will be a fluidic force that will represent the Essence of the entire personnel of the Brotherhood at any given time. This fluidic Correspondence of the Brotherhod will constitute a sort of Fluidic Brotherhood, which will be the exact duplicate of the Individualized Brotherhood, only it will act spontaneously and blindly, while the personal Brotherhood will act deliberately and consciously.

The sum total of these Magnetic Emanations will collectively form a sort of Hermetic Group Soul the diverse qualities of which will be derived from the diverse emanations in severalty, thus forming a general personality which will act in an objective manner, so to speak. This Personal Group Soul of the Brotherhood will react upon each member so as to transform his life and consciousness in accordance with its own nature. In this way it will constitute the Great Hermetic Mother, that will mold every member of the Brotherhood in accordance with the General Brotherhood Type. In this sense the Magnetic Counterpart of the Brotherhood will constitute the Hermetic Womb in which the soul of every Brother will be gestated and brought to birth. In this way the Magnetic Group Soul of the Brotherhood is the mother of all the Hermetic Brothers.

However, this is not all, the Magnetic Emanations that go to make up the completion of the Magnetic Group Soul act upon it in a direct manner, so that it is being transformed, and the state of the Group Soul at one time acts upon itself in a chemical manner so that it is continually evolving itself in accordance with the Laws of Creative Evolution. This means that the state of the Group Soul at one moment is giving birth to the state of the Group Soul of the next moment, i. e., the Group Soul is going through a continual process of reincarnation. The principle of the Indivisibility of Duration applies here the same as in the Kosmos itself. This results in the continual evolution of Self-Consciousness in the Group Soul. Thus we have the Spirit of the Brotherhood as an Objective Fact, apart from the personnel of the members of the physical Brotherhood.

We must also bear in mind the influence of the Karma produced by the Mentation of the members in the past. This accumulates and becomes the Kar-

mic Mind of the Brotherhood, and likewise the Group
Soul of the Brotherhood, so that for all practical
purposes, the Brothers of the past are all the time
present with the Brotherhood of the Present. The
Skhandas of one Brother are incarnate in another
so that we have the perpetuation of the Brotherhood
of the past in that of the present.

We must also bear in mind that the Group Soul
of the Brotherhood is ever striving to incarnate
in the Brothers of any Generation, and hence the
development of any one is in proportion to the degree in which this Group Soul is incarnate in him,
and he therefore ensouls it. From this it will be
seen that our development is not through the evolution of the Individual Soul, but rather through the
Individualization of the Group Soul of the Brotherhood. The standing of any one as a Hermetic
Brother is in exact ratio to the degree to which this
Group Soul has been able to become incarnate in
him.

This collective Group Soul was personified as
Hermes Trismegistus, and we as the sons of Hermes
Trismegistus are but the sons of the Hermetic Group
Soul. He is ever with us, and is the real head of
the Brotherhood for the reason that he is the Group
Soul of the Brotherhood. In a word, he is the Spirit
of the Brotherhood personified.

The Invisible Section of the Brotherhood is the
Skhandas of those members who have lived in the past,
manifesting their consciousness to those living in the
present, but they are in no sense of the word Spirit
Entities. The entire purpose of membership in the
Brotherhood is that one may be born of the Hermetic
Group Soul, and may become in this sense a true son
of Hermes Trismegistus. Membership in the Order
is not simply for the sake of association with other

students of Hermetic Philosophy, nor yet for the sake
of the Hermetic Initiations or the Instruction of the
Elder Brother; but above all this it is in order that we
may be brought into the Matrix which is provided by
the Hermetic Spirit or Group Soul, and there be transformed into the images of that Hermetic Spirit, and
in this way be Born Again as true Sons of Hermes,
partaking of the very Soul of Hermes, that is, we are
made to ensoul the Hermetic Spirit, which is thereby
enabled to ensoul our very being.

We may say from one point of view that this Hermetic Group Soul is the Soul of the Brotherhood, while
the membership of the Brotherhood at any period of
time constitutes the Body in which that Hermetic Soul
dwells.  It is in this sense that Thoth-Hermes is perpetually incarnated in the Hermetic Brotherhood, both
in the Hermetic Group Soul or Hermes Trismegistus
and also in the living membership of the Brotherhood.

## THE ATLANTEAN BROTHERHOOD.

The first appearance of the Hermetic Brotherhood was in Atlantis in the very beginning of the Atlantean Period; that is to say, it was organized in the first beginnings of the First Sub-Race of the Atlantean Root Race. The basis of the original Atlantean Religion, as the name Hermetic will indicate, was the worship of Kosmic Thought, and all the activities of Creative Evolution that flow from it. That is to say, they looked upon the Divine Reason or Intelligence as the Highest Conception of the Divine. To make the matter a little clearer, they held that in the highest sense Deity and Intelligence were identical, for Deity was Divine Ideation. This is not to be taken in the sense of a Personal Deity who was thinking, but rather in the sense of Pure Ideation as the Ultimate First Activity of all things. Out of this Primordial Divine Ideation, or Pure Ideation unconditioned, there developed a Centripetal Force that ever sought the Common Center of this Ideation. Thus there was developed a Self-Centering Activity that ever sought to bring the Circumference into the Center. Thus was Generated the Divine Self-Love, not the love between Subject and Object, for there was nothing but Divine Ideation, but rather the Love within the depths of Divine Ideation, the Love of each Ideative Activity and each Idea for the Principle of Pure Ideation itself, for they were one. Thus was born the Divine Love. Divinity can love nothing apart from itself, and it must love itself. From the excess of this Divine Love and Desire, this Desire which is incapable of Desiring anything apart from itself, for the reason that nothing else is Desirable to it, there grew a Resistance, a reaction upon itself, which engendered a tendency to flow forth, and give expression to itself. This resulted in a Centrifugal Force that flowed from the Center outward in Self-Expression. Thus was engendered the Will to make manifest the Idea, the Will to Self-Expression, and hence the Divine Will. This Divine Will is not the Will of a Personal God, but rather the Abstract Principle of Will, as the outflowing Will to become manifested, it is the Esse of the Ever Becoming, which is therefore the Manifesting Essence of Divine Ideation. It is the Ultimate Fiat of all things. Thus we have the Divine Trinity of Ideation, Desire and Will. This Will eventuates in the Creative Word, or the Formative Process which engenders all Form. Thus we have the Divine Conception which was the Root of all the other Divine Conceptions. This was the Basis of the Religion of the First Atlantean Sub-Race, the Yellow-White, or Moon Colored Race. There was no other Divine Conception save and except the Diverse Emanations from this Divine Ideative Principle.

The activity of the Ultimate Divine Reason, as Ideation, Desire, Will and the Creative Word, must in the nature of things specialize its own Substance in such a way as to form a lower kind of Substance, which is thus born out of the Divine Ideative Process, thus presenting the First Emanation from the Divine Ideative Substance. Thus we have the Primitive Kosmical Energy and Substance or Primeval Chaos. This Primeval Chaos is first of all the Void, where there is no activity, but only a great Stillness. This is Brooded upon by the Divine Will, and Motion is born within its depths. This Motion energizes every portion of the Kosmic Void, and it moves, becomes active, and thus is born Kosmic Energy. This Kosmic Energy from that time forth, forever energizes Kosmic Substance, so that the two are one, or rather the two aspects of the One, viz., the Dynamic Energy acting upon the Static Substance of the Kosmos, constituting the Active and Passive Principles of the Kosmos. From this time forth there is no longer any Primeval Chaos in the true sense of the word, for Primeval Chaos has become Kosmos. As a result of this activity within the Fullness of Kosmos, there is born forth a process of Kosmic Ideation similar to that of the Ultimate Ideation from which Kosmos came, the only difference being the Plane on which the Ideation is active. This process of Kosmic Ideation is the Kosmic Thinker or Thinking Substratum of the Kosmos. It is this which engenders all Kosmic

Thoughts. This Kosmic Ideation, as an Active Process, is Thoth-Hermes or Kosmic Thought. It was this Process that was deified as the Manifester of the Unmanifest Divine Ideation. This was deified as the Principle of Divine Conception in the time of the Second Sub-Race, the Golden Hued Race. During the Golden Age of Atlantis the People were worshipers of Kosmic Thought. The Hermetic Brotherhood was in a flourishing condition during this period, though it was not then a very Secret Order. In fact, the Mysteries were to a great extent public property. The Brotherhood was not so much for the purpose of instruction as it was for the purpose of training the soul in the living of the life and in the Incarnation in Form of the Truth which every one knew to a very great extent. It was not the Doctrine for which one entered the Brotherhood, but rather for the Worship and the Discipline. However, as in course of time the understanding of the nature of the Ultimate Divine Ideation began to become vague in the consciousness of the people, this had to be preserved in the Brotherhood, and therefore the First Secret Degree to be formed was what is now the Mystic Fourth Degree, for all that is now given in the Lower Degrees was the popular knowledge in the time of the Second Sub-Race.

However, there was a still farther development in the Religious and Philosophical Thought of that time. Kosmic Thought must in the very nature of things act upon Kosmic Substance and in this way specialize it unto certain definite ends. Thus will be started the beginning of the Differentiation of Substance which must eventuate in diverse processes of the Ever Becoming. In this way we will have two manifestations of this Specialized Activity, viz., that of Energy and that of Substance. The specialized state of Energy is the Kosmic Masculine, and the specialized state of Substance is the Kosmic Feminine, the interactivity of these two Forces is the cause of all the Mutations of Universal Substance, and hence the Esse of Creative Evolution. Out of the interrelation of the Kosmic Masculine and Feminine Principles was born Duration. Ever changing, subject to perpetual Mutations, and thus ever being reborn of the Womb of Female Vigor or the Great Mother, the Kosmic Virgin. Every moment of time the Kosmos as Duration is being Immaculately Conceived and at the same time Born of the Kosmic Virgin. Likewise at the same instant it dies, in order that it may enter the Womb of Duration and be Born Again. Thus is consummated the Eternal Redemption of the Kosmos. Through the Indivisibility of Duration all things are brought to completion. Universal Substance is Redeemed from its former state by death and rebirth into the next stage of perfection. This is the Hermetic Doctrine of the Crucified Christos, ever offered for the redemption of the Universe. It is the Universe itself dying at every moment that in the act of dying it may be reborn in its new relationship. Thus was formed the Cultus of the Great Mother as well as that of the Father of Gods and Men. It is this conception that has been misunderstood as Phallic Worship by the Early Atlanteans, though in the Black Atlanteans in some instances it did degenerate into that.

There also was another Divine Conception that was developed among this people, though it was not pronounced until the time of the Red Race. This was the conception of the Feathered Serpent. The Serpent is the Symbol of the Fire Principle. It is also the Kundalini Force in Man and also in the Universe. For that reason it becomes the Symbol of Life and also of Death, for Destruction is but the reversal of the process of Creation. It was in this sense the symbol of Creation and Destruction. It was likewise the Seminal Principle of the Manifested Universe, symbolizing, as it did, the Generation of all things. The Feathers were the symbol of the Air, relating, as they did, to the Bird. The Feathered Serpent was the Symbol, therefore, of all the Creative Forces of Creative Evolution that emanated from the Molding Activity of the Great Mother, and which operated through the Material Universe above the Physical Plane. These Creative Forces are the so-called Laws of Nature, the Super-Physical Forces that manifest the Activity of that Creative Mother Vigor, and which together engender the Physical Universe. However, He is not to be conceived as being a Chaos of such Forces, but is rather the Synthesis of all such Forces, externalizing through Matter the Activities of the Great Mother. It was during the time of the Red

Race that this Cultus of the Feathered Serpent became the dominant Religious Conception of Atlantis, and the result was the losing sight of the nature of Kosmic Thought and of the Father and Mother Energies of the Universe. To obviate this difficulty and in this way preserve the Ancient Knowledge, the Brotherhood made the teaching of those Truths secret, and thus there were during this time Three Secret Degrees in the Brotherhood, though the Cultus of the Feathered Serpent was popularly taught.

Among the Dark Atlanteans or the Fourth Sub-Race, the Mystery of the Feathered Serpent was lost sight of, and in lieu thereof the Cultus of Nature Worship, that is, the Worship of the Phenomena of Nature and the Physical Universe, was adopted. They had become so material that they saw only the Physical. Thus Magnetism of the Terrestrial Order was accepted in place of the Celestial Magnetism and the Astral and Mental Water and Air. The result of this was that in the course of time it became essential for the Mystery of the Feathered Serpent to be withdrawn from the People, and thus the Fourth Degree of the Brotherhood was formed. That is, it was the Fourth in process of formation, though it was the First into which anyone must enter, and hence the name of it was the First Degree. In this Degree was taught the Mystery of the Feathered Serpent. One reason for making this Knowledge secret, however, was the fact that the Dark Race were sure to use the knowledge contained therein for Magical purposes, and it was thought best to permit them to entirely lose sight of the Truth with reference to the Higher Kosmical Currents of Force rather than that they should use it for the purposes of Practical Occultism. The withdrawal of the Mystery of the Feathered Serpent from the people soon precipitated their sinking entirely into the realm of the Physical, and at last there was no knowledge beyond the Physical Plane and the Forces belonging thereto. In this way it came about that in the course of time the Atlantean Brotherhood disappeared from Poseidonis altogether, and was to be found only on the shores of North America and the other countries into which it had been introduced by the Mayas. The Brotherhood that was on Poseidonis at the time it went down was not the

Ancient Brotherhood at all, but rather a Brotherhood of Practical Occultists. They practised the Hermetic Art, but know very little of Hermetic Science, and nothing at all of Hermetic **Philosophy.**

The True Hermetic Brotherhood perpetuated all the Ancient Knowledge as well as the Ancient Spirit of the perished Races of Atlantis, and not only did they conserve the Ancient Truths, but they also Incarnated them, and thus there was at all times a body of the Elect, who preserved in their own lives and consciousness the Golden Age of Atlantis, but this they could not give to the others, and for that reason the Hermetic Mysteries of the Golden Past became a Sealed Book to all but the few who were admitted to the Sacred Temples. This will explain the terrible war that was waged upon the Red Atlanteans by the Dark Race. It was well known to the Dark Race that the Red Race had amongst them men who were Initiates into the Deepest Mysteries of the Feathered Serpent and the Great Mother, and as such they were the Greatest Masters of Arcane Knowledge in the world. Therefore the Black Emperor waged incessant war on the White Emperor with the hope of getting the Elder Brothers into his hands and forcing them to disclose the Arcane Word which they held. If they could only gain the Lost Word and the Lost Chord that were in the hands of the White Brotherhood, they would be the masters of the World. However, they were never able to get very many of them into their clutches, and those who did fall into their hands had the courage to die on the Sacrificial Stone rather than give the Master's Word to the profane and the unworthy. At last the terrible Curse of the Elder Brothers went home, and Poseidonis, being entirely in the hands of the Dark Race, was sent to the bottom of the Ocean. But the Master's Word continued to be spoken among the White Atlanteans in America, among the Mayas, Quiches, Toltecs, Egyptians, Akkadians, and some other peoples. And that Word will never become entirely silent so long as life endures on the earth.

## THE MAYA BROTHERHOOD.

The Red Atlanteans who settled in Yucatan being members of the Hermetic Brotherhood of Atlantis, it followed naturally that the Brotherhood should be perpetuated among the Mayas. However, they gave a special trend to the Evolution of the Brotherhood such as it had never had in Atlantis. To them the all important Divine Principle was the Mother of the Gods, or the Great Mother, Female Vigor par excellence. This was quite natural for a people expressing that particular degree of Spirituality. They were no longer on the plane where they could adequately understand the Mystery of the Heart of Heaven or even its lowest aspect, Kosmic Thought. To them the all-important Mystery was that of the Generation of the Kosmos, hence the beginning of Kosmogenesis was the subject of their deepest veneration. Taking a somewhat practical view of the matter, it was not so much the Energy which was the Ultimate expression of this process as the Substance which molded and gave expression and form to the Kosmos. This being the case, it was inevitable that they should look more to the principle of Kosmic Motherhood that engendered the first manifestations of evolving life. It was not the Ultimate or Primordial World, the World of Ideas, that they were interested in, but rather the World of Form, of which they were a part. However, it must not be understood by this that they reverenced the Physical World, for that would be misleading; it was rather the realm of causation that eventuated in the Sensible World. It was not the Unmanifest, but rather the Manifestation, that they worshiped, but at the same time it was the Process of Manifestation rather than the Manifested State.

The Great Mother is the Molding Process which is ever going on in the Akasa, thus giving Form to it, and at the same time continually reforming it. She is not that which has given birth to the Universe, but rather that which is ever giving birth to it. This perpetual rebirth is made possible owing to the perpetual transformation that is going on all the time. Nothing is ever perfected, but rather every moment of time

is the Process of the Ever Becoming. The Great
Mother is at every moment of time bringing into manifestation that which is her own state of attainment at
that particular moment. When we realize that this
activity in the Female Vigor, or Kosmic Substance, engenders a state of Consciousness which is the Intelligent aspect of that very state of activity—and thus she
is Self-Conscious with a Self-Consciousness exactly
corresponding to the State of Activity going on within
her—we can realize that this Self-Consciousness reacts
upon her Substance so as to determine the Mode of its
Activity, and thus the nature of the Formative process
which it will express. Therefore this Mother Substance is ever transforming itself, so that it becomes
the realization of its previous state of Self-Consciousness. This, therefore, means that It is evolving Itself.
At the same time that it does this, it is giving form to
its own Substance and thus is giving birth to certain
Modes of Activity, which are in reality specializations
of this very Substance, and which constitute the first
beginnings of Manifest Existence. It is thus that the
Great Mother is ever giving Birth to a Universe which
at the moment of its birth is the exact expression of
the Consciousness of the Great Mother, and yet in the
very act of giving Birth to that Universe the Substance
of the Great Mother has gone through a Transformation which has made her a slight degree in advance of
the Universe she has given birth to. Her experience of
Motherhood is therefore the means of her Evolution.
Not only is this true, but this new Mode of Activity,
with its accompanying Self-Consciousness, acts upon
the Substance of the Form which she has given Birth
to, so that it is transformed in accordance with the new
state of the Great Mother, and thus it is procreated
and born again in accordance with that new state.
From this it will be seen that the Universe is every
moment being reborn and also is at all times gestating
in the Womb of the Great Mother. The Substance of
the Great Mother is ever taking Form as the Universe,
and at the same time being resolved back into the state
of the Great Mother. The question then is, How can
the same Substance be at one and the same time the
Great Mother of the Universe and likewise the Universe itself? This becomes plain when we bear in mind

that the Great Mother is not a certain quantity of Substance separate from all other Substance, but is rather
the Formative Molding process within Substance, the
Universe being the Form which it takes at any given
moment.  To make the matter a little clearer, the Great
Mother is the Tendency to Mold, while the Universe is
the Process of being Molded.  It is this distinction
alone which marks the separation of the Universe from
the Great Mother who is ever engendering it.

As a result of this Formative Activity of the Great
Mother, there are certain specialized Modes of Activity
which are in reality but so many differentiations of
that Formative Process.  Each one of these specialized
Modes of Activity preserves its own identity with reference to every other such Mode, and yet the Formative Activity of the Great Mother so specialized is ever
changing, so that the same transformation that is going on in the Great Mother Process is also going on in
her Modes, so that there is in these Modes of Activity
a Creative Evolutionary Process exactly analogous to
that which is going on in the Great Mother herself.
These specialized Modes of Activity are called the
Gucumatz, the Serpents with Dazzling Azure Wings.
These Gucumatz are the Kundalini Forces of the Kosmos, or the Creative Fires, hence the Fiery Serpents of
the Mysteries.  They are likewise the Gestative Fires
in the Womb of the Great Mother.  They are all specialized manifestations of the Kosmic Fire.  It is these
Forces which are spoken of as the Fires of the Universe, that is, the Fires out of which the Universe is
engendered.  They are the Consuming Fire of Rider
Haggard, the Rosicrucian Fire, the Fire of the Heart
of Nature, the Fire of Life and likewise the Fire Mist
of Science.  The Sacred Fire of the Temple was the
Symbol of those Serpents of Fire, each Fire symbolizing one of the Fiery Serpents.  Likewise are the Altar
Lamps their symbols, except in the case where they
symbolize the Lights which have either a higher or a
lower meaning than the Creative Fires.  The Sacred
Fire was never permitted to go out for the reason that
the Gucumatz must never cease their life of Perpetual
Mutation.  The Sacred Fires were attended by Virgins whose duty it was to tend the Sacred Fire and see
that it never went out.  They were women for the rea-

son that the Gucumatz were the Creative Fires of the Great Mother, and, as they were Feminine, they must be tended by women. The meaning of this was that in the Kosmos it was the Mother Principle of the Great Mother acting through them that ever renewed them and kept them burning. They were virgins for the reason that, having never known a man, they were the fit symbol of the Feminine Essence of the Great Mother that was expressing itself in that way. They were not Masculine Fires, but, from the Maya conception, Feminine Fires, and were but the modes of manifestation of that Mothering process. Another thing that was symbolized here was the application of this Mystery to the Individual. In this sense, the Guardian of the Sacred Fire was feeding it within her own soul, and in this sense she must be a virgin, for only by the conservation of the Feminine Sex Magnetism could the Fire of the Soul be kept burning, and thus the lower nature be ever regenerated. The Keeper of the Sacred Fire dressd in a special manner. She wore a loose Loin Cloth or skirt falling from the waist to a point just above the knees, and a Sacrificial Apron over the front part of the body from the waist to a point just high enough to cover the breasts. The Loin Cloth was Green, to symbolize the Earth, for water is the symbol of the Feminine Substance wherever it may be found. When water has descended in the form of rain and has watered the earth, it causes the earth to bring forth vegetation, which is in reality water in the form of vegetation. This is Green in color and covers the earth with a mantle of Green, hence in this sense Green is the symbol of the Mother Principle manifesting through Physical Matter. For this reason Green symbolizes Water wherever it may be found. The Green Skirt is therefore the symbol of the Mother Principle in the Earth. Also the figure from the waist down is the symbol of the Earth, while from the waist up it symbolizes the Sky, or that which is above the Physical Plane. The Green Cloth covers all of that part of the body suggesting Generation, which indicates that the Sacred Fires are lost in the generation of matter, and therefore are not Fire but Water on that plane. Blue is the color of the Sky, and hence is the symbol of the Airy Region between the Water and the Fire. This covers those parts of the body that are connected with the elements of Motherhood above the waist line; that is, according to the mysteries, in the Airy Region. The locality of the Womb and Uterus as well as the Breasts, which are associated with the nursing of the child after birth, are covered with the Apron of Air. The meaning of this is that as the Gucumatz are Fiery, they cease to be the Gucumatz as soon as they pass below the level of the Fire, and therefore they become something else. These Sacred Fires do not Generate on those planes, but rather they engender that which generates there. Again, they are not in reality the Generatrix, but are the modes of Generation of the Generatrix. The penalty for permitting the Sacred Fires to go out is death, for if the Gucumatz were to cease to operate the Universe would cease to be, and if those Fires die out in the Soul the soul will cease to be.

The Gucumatz in their activity tend to the production of Unity of Action. Out of the totality of their specialized activities there is born a synthesized activity making for Unity. This united activity results in a living, active, self-conscious, creative process. A process that is ever changing, yet ever the same, for it is the consequence of the united action of the Gucumatz. This is the Synthesized Fire resulting from the synthetic action of all the diverse Creative Fires. It is the Process of the Ever Becoming in the absolute sense. This is the Universe, as the Child of the Great Mother, the Child that is ever being born, and at the same time ever Gestating in the Womb of the Great Mother, for it is at once the synthesis of the Fires and that which results from the synthesis. It is at once the Creative Evolutionary Process and also that which is Created and Evolved. This is Kukulkan, or the Feathered Serpent. The Serpent represents the Fire and the Feathers the Air. Thus the Feathered Serpent is this Creative Evolutionary Process, or rather the Form which it assumes on the Plane of Fire and Air. The Azure Wings of the Gucumatz also represent the element of Air, and the meaning is that the Gucumatz are merged and lost in the Feathered Serpent. In a word, they cease to be the Gucumatz and become the Feathered Serpent, or the Universe. The Feathered Serpent is supposed to be Masculine, though in reality he includes the Feminine element within himself. He is the Universe above the Physical Plane. In the latter He becomes in a great measure Fixed, so that the form changes again.

On the Physical Plane or, to speak more accurately, in the Etheric Region, the forces of the Feathered Serpent take a more stable form and become the Great Macow Bird that descends from the Heavens to the Earth. This great Macow Bird is the Universe in the form of Physical Ether, and is the Fabricator that, out of its own nature, fabricates the World of Gross Matter. This Principle is both Male and Female, having the two sexes in a state of balance. It is but the expression of the Feathered Serpent on the Physical Octave.

The activities of the Great Macow become fixed in Votan, the Gross Physical Universe, but as this is but the fabricated result of the Fabricating Process going on in the Great Macow it follows that the Earth, or Votan, is in a process of continual change, or Evolution.

The Great Macow was the Patron Goddess of the Queen, for the reason that the Queen was supposed to embody the Feminine aspect of the Fabricator, and to be the Fabricatrix of the Nation, therefore her Totem was the Macow, just as the National Standard was the Feathered Serpent. The meaning of this latter symbolism was that the Mayas as a people must change as the Feathered Serpent changed, and must in fact at all times ensoul the Feathered Serpent at that particular moment; thus they must evolve with the Universe. Therefore the Mayas were, to all intents and purposes, the Universe.

When the High Priest went into the Sanctuary to consult the gods he always went naked, for in their presence he was not a priest but a supplicant. He was, in fact, the representative of the people, and stood in their presence devoid of all covering and of all ornament, for he must bring his naked soul to them if he was to know their will. When he went forth to declare the will of the gods to the people, he went as the representative of the gods, whom all must obey, hence he was the High Priest, and therefore he dressed in all his Sacerdotal Vestments, as became the messenger of the Gods.

They offered human sacrifices, and in this way symbolized the fact that it is only by dying on the Plane of the Manifested that we can return to the Bosom of the Divine Mother. This Rite also taught that those who thus die on the lower planes and enter the state of the Great Mother exercise a Vicarious influence on human life below, thus tending to lift the Race Spirit up in the direction of the Great Mother. It was never believed there was any Vicarious efficacy in the Sacrifice itself; it was rather the idea of symbolizing in the form of a sacrificial death on the Physical Plane the Mystic Death, or Living Death, of the Sacred Person who undertook to kill out the Generative Processes that were going on in him below the level of the Great Mother. As this was a symbol of the Mystic Death, few Human Sacrifices were offered, only enough to keep the Idea of Vicarious Living Sacrifice alive in the consciousness of the people. It may be farther stated that in the original Mayan Religion there were no Human Sacrifices, but only the Living Deaths, but as time went by they lost sight of the original meaning of the Mystery and began to symbolize it by the actual offering of Blood Sacrifices. This in time tended to some extent to hide the Spiritual Meaning of the Rite altogether.

Their Mysticism was largely Mathematical and Geometrical in its Symbolism. Their most Sacred Numbers were 3, 5, 7, 9 and 13. The meaning of these Numbers will be clear to all who are versed in Occult Mathematics and will unveil the inner meaning of much of their Mysteries as well as their Hieroglyphics. Nine is the number of the Hermetic Ogdoad with Kosmic Thought or Thoth at the head of it. With the Mayas this position was occupied by the Heart of Heaven as the First, the Father and the Mother of the Gods as the Second and Third, the Feathered Serpent polarized as Male and Female as the Fourth and Fifth, the Great Macow, both male and female, as Sixth and Seventh, and Votan polarized as male and female as Eighth and Ninth. Nine was also the number of Gestation of the Foetus and therefore symbolized the Gestation and Birth of the Feathered Serpent.

## THE AKKADIAN BROTHERHOOD.

The Mayas who settled in Akkad were all members of the Mayan Brotherhood, and hence it was only natural that they should bring over with them the Hermetic Teaching of their countrymen. In this way they perpetuated in Akkad the ancient Mayan Mysteries, though not in their original purity. We do not, for instance, find any allusion to the Heart of Heaven in any of its aspects, which goes to show that they were not familiar with the highest aspect of the Mayan Teaching. This, however, was largely due to the fact that those who settled there were not Initiates of what is now the Fourth Degree of the Brotherhood, but knew only the three lower Degrees.

The highest gods known to the Akkadians were Anu and his wife Ishtar. Anu corresponds to Osiris and is the Father of the Gods as well as of Nature. Ishtar was the same as Isis or the Great Mother. Thus the two highest gods were the two aspects of Duration, or Space as the Engendering Principle of all things. Ishtar was the Formative Process in Nature, that is to say, she was Nature acting in this Formative Capacity. The diverse Transformations and Mutations of Universal or Kosmic Substance ever tended to Engender the Universe. Thus we have the Process of Creative Evolution ever bringing out of itself that which is to be, hence the Process of the Ever Becoming was figured as the basis of all that is or is to be. Ishtar was therefore the Gestative Process in Kosmos that is ever bringing forth Kosmos. She was, hence, not only the Gestative Process but also the Synthetic Process, hence the Process of Unification, as well as the binding and uniting tendency in Kosmos, that which transforms Chaos into Kosmos, and at the same time is perpetually renewing Kosmos, so as to bring forth out of the Kosmos that which is to be engendered. In this respect the Akkadian Conception of Ishtar was identical with the Maya Conception of the Mother of the Gods.

This Synthetic Process can be possible only through the engendering of an Attractive or Gravitative Principle, which causes all of the diverse activities of Kosmos to seek each the other, and thus bring about an Integration of all of those tendencies and hence of all the atoms of Kosmic Substance. Thus there is engendered a Magnetic Attraction among all the diverse elements engendered by the activity of the Formative Process. This attraction is in reality the Principle of Love. Just as love between persons is the Principle of Chemical Affinity that draws them together and makes for unity between them, particularly between two persons of opposite sex, so is the same principle working among the Kosmic Elements, and in the same way making for unity among them; that is, the Centripetal Force that causes them to seek a common Center of Gravity and thus gather around a common nucleus, what we may term Kosmic Love, and it is the same kind of love in the Universe that brings about unity among men and women. In this way it appears that the source of Kosmic Love, that is the love among the Kosmic Elements, is in the Formative Activity of the Great Mother Principle. It is through this love—that is, Mutual Attraction—that formation is made possible. This Love or Mutual Attraction is also the origin of Chemical Affinity. In this way Ishtar becomes the Goddess of Love and Sex Attraction.

Anu and Ishtar are the two poles of the same principle, Anu operating through Energy and Ishtar through Substance. All of the Life activities in nature are the result of the combined activity of Anu and Ishtar in the engendering of this attraction, though Anu operates rather in the direction of separation, while Ishtar operates in the direction of unification. In individual life, Anu dominates the Life Energy while Ishtar dominates the Material Form, though this is not to be taken with reference to the Physical Form alone.

It is Ishtar operating in the human that causes the desire for offspring and also for the companionship of the opposite sex. She acts upon the Emotional Nature of woman and engenders within the woman the desire for Motherhood. It is the workings of the Molding Process in woman that awakens in her the desire to mold and to bring forth, for that process has begun within her inward principles and has affected her Sex Energy even in her Physical Body, so as to cause it to act formatively. In a word, the formative activity has already begun to transform her sex force and thereby to awaken her sex organs to activity. This maternal activity, which is absolutely independent of the volition of the woman, acting as it does from the time of her maturity, and as the direct result of the Formative Process, awakens in her the natural desire for the opposite sex element, so that she may bring forth that which she is striving to form. It is in this way that sex desire is awakened as the working of the Principle of Kosmic Motherhood. In proportion as a woman is more feminine so does this force operate the stronger in her, and so does the desire for offspring, and hence the desire for a mate, grow upon her. This same force operates upon the man also, and the result is the impulse to give life, and the impulse to give form brings the two together. It is in this way that the Formative Process operating in two forms of opposite polarity brings them together through the impulse to find the other element necessary to create. This impulse to create is the product of the Formative Process operating in the two of them. For this reason it follows that all sex attraction is the work of the Formative Process operating in the bodies and souls of the ones drawn together. All cases of falling in love are the operation of this principle. It is for this reason that Ishtar becomes the Goddess of Love and Sex Attraction. She is therefore the Goddess of Marriage and Parentage. But realizing that she dominates all sex conjunctions, we must see that she does not confine herself to the marriage relation, but operates in and through others so as to lead to this act independent of the sanction of the marriage relation. All sexual relations are under her patronage whether the parties be married or not. This becomes clear when we realize that she is the Formative and Engendering Process in Nature and acts upon all Nature in this way. The Sex Instinct is therefore the workings of Ishtar, no matter in what relation it operates. Adultery was therefore as much her act as was legalized sex relations, and from the standpoint of the religious element here involved there was nothing sinful in the adulterous action, for was it not an act in response to the promptings of Ishtar? And were they not, in fact, giving expression to her nature?

In many instances this led to the idealizing of lust, for was not all lust awakened by her? And were they not therefore doing an act of worship to her if they complied with her impulses? The worshipers of Ishtar concluded that the marriage relation was a scheme to regulate and control the activities of Ishtar, and that was regarded as impious, hence the one who refused to abide the restraining influences of the home and insisted upon freedom to express their sex impulses whenever and wherever they were felt, was regarded as a more devout disciple of Ishtar than the others.

Her Priestesses were all Courtesans who served their Mistress by giving up their bodies for the sexual uses of the worshipers, and such relation with the Sacred Courtesans was regarded as the most holy of all the acts of worship to the Goddess, for these Sacred Courtesans were in a certain sense assumed to represent Ishtar herself, and hence relation with them was taken as relation with the Goddess. Thus the worship of Ishtar became more in the nature of sexual intercourse in her honor than anything else.

At the same time there were those among the higher Initiates who realized that this was not the true worship of Ishtar. They held that she operated within as well as without, and that the formative and creative activity of the Goddess could transpire on the Inner Planes of being, and it would therefore be as much the expression of Ishtar as it was when it transpired in the outer. Those Initiates realized that the true worship of Ishtar was in the restraining of sex expression in the outer, so that the transformation might go on within the inner nature, and in this way they might be born again from time to time. Thus the inner union with Ishtar was the Spiritual Worship, which was only symbolized in a gross physical manner by the Exoteric Worship.

The Formative activity of Ishtar under the impulse of Anu was perpetually engendering Kosmos, which was also under the perpetual transformations of Creative Evolution. In a word, it was the ever-changing and evolving course of Nature, the same as the Mayas presented under the symbol of the Feathered Serpent. This all-mutative course of Nature was the god Bel, who was the Son of Ishtar ever being engendered, and ever dying in order that he might be born again. He was also the Man of the Sun, the Sun being used as his symbol, for as the Sun regulates the course of Nature in our world through his movements, so Bel regulates the course of Nature in all Space by reason of his ever-transforming state.

As Bel is this ever-changing course of Nature under the impulse of Creative Evolution, ever dying that he may be born again, it follows that he can only evolve and progress by manifesting the fruitage of his past state in his present state. In a word, the selfhood of Bel must pass over into the Selfhood that is to be, his past must live in his present manifestation. As a Buddhist would say, the Karma of Bel's past must live in and determine his present. This was symbolized in the offering of jars and vases to him. The jars and the vases being the receptacles of and for his past, just as the same vase or bowl was in the funeral rite the receptacle for the good deeds of the deceased. When one made the offering of a bowl, jar or vase he in effect said, "may thy past achievements live in thy present manifestations." The hope of the world for progress depended entirely upon the ability of Bel to thus evolve His New Self out of the Old Selfhood.

Next below Bel, and growing out of his activity, was Inlil, the Lord of Lands, hence the same as Votan, or the Generative Masculine Virility of the Earth, which was the manifestation of the mutations of Bel through the Physical Energy of the Earth.

His consort was Ninlil, Mistress of Heaven and Earth, or the feminine aspect of Inlil. She was the physical counterpart of Ishtar, and the manifestation through the physical substance of the earth of the mutations of Bel, being dominated absolutely by him. She was in fact the Formative or Gestative Process in the Earth, and hence the equivalent of Pachamama, the Feminine aspect of Votan. It was the confusion of Ishtar with Ninlil that led to the inchastity connected with the worship of the former Goddess, for Ishtar was at all times above the plane of the Sensible World. The Mystery that was taught to the Initiates was the distinction between Ishtar and Ninlil. However, the true nature of Ninlil did not justify physical inchastity, for she was Kosmical and not personal.

From the foregoing it will appear that the Religion of the Akkadians was a form of Kosmogony Deified, and it was similar to that of the Mayas, with the exception that it was not quite so philosophical in its nature and that nothing was known of the Pure Spiritual Region. It was, in fact, nothing but the deification of Creative Evolution. Furthermore, it was far more realistic and less idealistic than was that of the Mayas.

Their system was to a great extent a Feminism, similar to that of the Mayas, but owing to the fact that marriage was less sacred than the position of the Free Courtesan this Feminism was not so prominent in the home life as it was among the Mayas. In a word, the married woman was far more under the control of her husband than she was among the Mayas, while the Feminine authority was vested in the hands of the Sacred Courtesans, for they were looked upon as the embodiments of Ishtar. This arrangement led to the elevation of the Sacred Courtesan to the position of the most honored of women. She was in reality the very expression of the Divine Feminine.

Thus we have in the Akkadians the first expression of that process of materializing the Mysteries that has been witnessed in so many instances since that time.

There is another aspect of the problem which must not be lost sight of. The most important element of this teaching was the descent of the Spirit into Matter, and hence it is that it is the expression of the Sex Force of the Great Mother in all of its manifestations through the Material Aspect that the Material Evolution is brought about. Likewise, in a system which expressed the Spiritual Evolution of the Material upward this same sex force would have to be spiritualized and lifted upward from the Material to the Spiritual Pole of manifestation. This is the real explanation for the two tendencies in the Mystery cults.

## THE CHALDEAN BROTHERHOOD.

The Akkadians being members of the Hermetic Brotherhood, it follows that as they settled Upper Chaldea and became the Chaldeans, or rather their descendants did, they continued in the same Religion, and hence were Hermetic also. The Chaldean Brotherhood was merely the Chaldean Section of the Akkadian Brotherhood. Hence the gods that were worshipped by the Akkadians and the Chaldeans were identical. So far as the fundamentals of the religion were concerned there was no difference between the Akkadians and the Chaldeans. The only essential differences were in the application of the Teaching and in the form in which it was presented.

Bel being the Way, or the Course of Nature, in the sense of the Course of Creative Evolution, and in this sense the Universe, it followed that whatever was connected with the Course of Creative Evolution in the Universe was to them an object of worship. As the Universe was seen to operate through the movements of the Stars, it became inevitable that they would see in the movements of the stars in their courses the Modes of Bel's operations, and hence the manner in which the Universal Process of Causation was operative. Astrology was therefore destined to become one of the principal branches of Chaldean Theology, because of its relation to the process of Causation so far as the Universal Manifestation was concerned. Thus was developed the idea of looking upon the motions of the Heavenly Bodies as the actions of Bel. Bel being the Way, it followed that all His actions were Divine, hence whatever channel He moved through was Divine. In this way the motion of the Stars became a Divine Mode of Action, and the Stars themselves became Divine. In the course of time they reached the point where to them every star was a god, in the sense that it was a Mode of the Action of Bel. The Sun became Bel himself for the reason that it was the motion of the Sun that regulated the motions of the Solar System. Thus they say Bel is the Sun. Because of the relation which Moonlight bears to Sunlight the Moon soon came to be looked upon as the

consort of the Sun, and therefore as the consort of Bel.
In the course of time they forgot the true relation of
Bel to Ishtar, for she was no longer recognized as His
Mother, and because of the fact that Bel was known
to be the perpetual Form through which the Formative activity of Ishtar was operating, He to a certain
extent became identified with her, and thus as the
Manifestation of Ishtar he was Ishtar. The inevitable
result was that Ishtar was degraded into a sort of
Feminine Bel, and therefore she became his consort,
and therefore the Moon Goddess. In the popular Religion of the country Bel was simply the Sun and Ishtar the Moon, but to the Initiates of the Brotherhood
Bel was still the same as the Feathered Serpent, and
Ishtar was His Syzygy or Feminine Counterpart, and
to the Initiates of the Third Degree Her true relation
as His Mother was understood, but to no one else.
All this led to the Deification of Astrology, and thus
we have in the Chaldean Brotherhood the first beginning of Esoteric Astrology.

The next branch of the Sacred Science was the
Science of Numbers. They understood the meaning of
Sacred Numbers, as being the Science on which all
things were founded. To understand the meaning of
this we must bear in mind that all things are Modes
of Motion. The Synthesis of all the Modes is Bel
Himself, and all the Modes of Motion are but the
Modes of Bel's activity. Motion, in order to be Creative, must move in accordance with Rhythm, and the
essence of Rhythm is Number. Number is but another
name for Order, for the beginning of Order is the or-
dering of all Motion, that is, the moving in accordance
with Number. The nine digits are the nine great
modes of activity which spring directly out of the
Gestative Action of Ishtar, and are manifested through
Bel. They are therefore the nine Formative Modes
which are the Matrix of all Formation. Each of these
numbers is in reality but Rhythm engendering a specific form of Formative Action.

1 is the Unity of Motion, from which nothing can
arise.

2 is the Duality of Motion, which is the first beginning of Differentiation.

3 is the Balance of the two contending Forces, which awakens the Creative Potencies.

4 is the Rhythm growing out of the Balance of Opposition, which must be the Matrix of all Formation.

5 is the Balance expressing itself through the Duality, and thus tending to the expression of Creative Life.

6 is the union of the Double Balance and hence the Union which must bring into being all Organic Manifestation; it is that which binds together.

7 is the union of 3 and 4, and hence the Balance manifesting through Rhythm, unto the giving of birth to the diverse modes of action.

8 is the double Rhythm, hence the double Formation, which engenders the double Form.

9 is the Triple Triangle, that is, it is the Dual Balance balanced by the Triad, and hence the completion of Formative Action which brings into being all of the Specialized Modes of Action.

The diverse combinations of these Nine Holy Numbers, together with the O or Matrix of No-Thing, gives to us all the differentiations of Creative Activity. This being the case, every conceivable combination of numbers will correspond to some combination of the Creative Force, and hence to some Creative Activity. This being the case, the specific nature of every Creative Mode of Action can be ascertained through the Number which corresponds to it. Occult Mathematics, therefore, becomes the Science of Creative Evolution. All the Mutations of Bel can be worked out Mathematically. It was for this reason that Mathematics became one of the Sacred Sciences. The meaning of all the diverse Numbers was worked out and tabulated, and this record constituted the Chaldean Book of Numbers. From this has been derived the Mathematical Kabbala of the Jews. Language is but the result of certain combinations of letters to form words, and the use of these words to express the thoughts that are back of them. A word therefore has two meanings. The Mathematical meaning, which is derived from the numerical value of the letters which go to compose it, and which therefore indicates the particular combination of Creative Forces, hence the Specific Mode of Creative Action to which it relates, and hence a meaning which can never be changed, for it is fixed in the very constitution of the Universe. This was the origin of the Literal Kabala. One who understands this Mathematical Language can never make a mistake as to the meaning of a word when it is used with reference to the Creative Powers of Nature. All Scriptures must be used in accordance with this Mathematical Key. Thus there grew up the Chaldean Science of Language, which was the third of the Sacred Sciences. There is also the popular meaning of the word, which changes with usage, and is of no value in Philosophy save to veil the Mysteries from the Profane.

The Diverse Modes of Creative Activity each move along their own particular Angle; thus we have diverse Lines of Force, giving rise to diverse Forms of action, which is the origin of Occult Geometry and in this way was developed Geometry as the fourth of the Sacred Sciences.

All of those Sciences dealing with the diverse aspects of the law of Motion, it follows that the Science of Motion per se, or Metaphysics, became the fifth of the Sacred Sciences.

Chemistry, or the Material Combinations growing out of the Creative Activity, constituted the sixth of the Sacred Sciences.

Psychology, including the Nabathean Agriculture, constituted the seventh of the Sacred Sciences.

However, it is to be borne in mind that the most important of all the Sacred Sciences was Magic. Mag in Chaldean means man, the same as Mac in Mayan. Magus therefore means The Man, or the Manful One. The Magi are the Men par excellence, and therefore Magic is Manhood. In a word, the Magical Agent was the Masculine Will, and Magic was the Art of making use of that Will Force in a Scientific Manner. The Magic Potency of the Will was systematically cultivated, and its exercise was the eighth of the Sacred Sciences. It was through Will Force alone that the Magic Power was exercised. One of the lowest forms of this Magic Power is what is now termed Hypnotism or Mesmerism. Another form of it is Animal Magnetism. Christian Science is another aspect of the same Force. Telepathy and all of the diverse Yoga Powers are but aspects of the Magic Potency of the Will, and so is Alchemy. All the miracles of the diverse Scriptures are but the results of this same Magic, that is, the systematic use of the latent Will Force in one for the accomplishment of the desired results. In later times Magic became degraded into a form of Invocation or Evocation and use of Elemental Forces in such a way as to be united with them, but the true Magical Agent is the Latent Potency of the Will.

The Chaldean Oracles present a very accurate idea of the ancient Chaldean Religion and Philosophy. Bel being the Great God of the Chaldeans, it proves that they were in the main only Initiated into the Second Degree of the Brotherhood, and that only a few of the Elect were admitted into the Third Degree, where they learned the Mystery of Ishtar or the Great Mother. Scarcely any of them were Initiated into the Fourth Degree, hence we find no trace of the conception of the Heart of Heaven among them, yet there were a few in the early days of their existence who in reality understood the Mystery of the Heart. It is useless to depend upon the researches of Scientists for information about their Religion, for the reason that they were all Members of the Hermetic Brotherhood, that is the Priesthood were, and therefore all of their Higher Teaching was presented under the cloak of the Hermetic Symbolism. Totemism was one of the most fundamental branches of their Sacred Mysteries. The Chaldean Brotherhood was founded about 12,000 B. C. This being the case, the Chaldeans of the historical period were sadly degenerated and do not represent the real Chaldeans at all.

## THE EGYPTIAN BROTHERHOOD.

When the Mayas came into Egypt they found a people there with a religion founded upon Sex in the strictest sense of the word, the very root of their religion being the Cultus of the Great Mother. This must not, however, be confused with the Philosophical Cultus current among the Mayan peoples, for it was derived more from the phenomenal presentation of Nature. They used the Lunar Calendar, though in former times they had used the Stellar Calendar, and much of their Mythology was based upon the movements of the stars. During the long ages that they had been in the country, and also in earlier times when they were in Lybia and Aethiopia, they had gone through several transformations in the Cultus, which at all times had been a Feministic Cultus. The first and earliest form of the Divine Conception was that of the Seven Stars, as the Fixer of Time, and the Turner Back, in the sense of the Regulator of the Changes and Transformations of Nature. Out of this grew the conception of Kaf the Generatrix, who was supposed to generate all forms of life from her own substance. In this conception we have the realization of the beginning of Creative Evolution, for Kaf is simply the Formative Aspect of Space, though this was not so Abstract in their conception. As Kaf was associated with the Seven Stars in certain forms of the Cultus, it is evident they assumed that the motions of the Stars determined the mode of activity of this Formative Principle which they called Kaf or the Generatrix. From this it is seen that in the first aspect of the subject Kaf was more physical than anything else. All things were supposed to come forth from Kaf the Generatrix; she had no husband but all was the result of the gestative activity of the Formative Principle. In other words, this Formative Activity acted in a mechanical way under the influence of the Stars; thus it did not require any fecundating male principle. Therefore there was no Male God in their conception, but all was the work of Kaf.

Then, in the course of time, there grew up the realization that as things were formed they would not as yet be perfect, but more in the nature of Germs from which the things that were to be the ultimate Forms were to grow, and this led to the natural result of all the Forms generated by Kaf being in the nature of Growing States that must be nourished in some way and thus permitted to attain their growth. So there developed the idea that this Formative Principle of Creative Evolution was not only the Generatrix of every thing, but also Kefa, the Suckler, who gave of her substance to those Forms that as Kaf she had engendered. From this it will be seen that Kaf and Kefa are but two aspects of the same Principle and that they relate, respectively, to the Formative Principle as the Engenderer of all Form and as the Feeder or Nourisher of those Forms after they have been Engendered. The Totem of Kaf was the Hippopotamus, and that of Kefa the Sow, for she was the Deo-Multimammea. But there was developed also the idea that there was inherent in this same Formative and Nourishing Principle, a Principle of Disintegration. Thus there was at war with Kefa, the Nourisher or Suckler, a Devouring Principle that tended to reduce every thing back to the state of the original substance from which it had been derived. This was called Matet-Eater of Millians, for she was supposed to devour all that was generated. She was represented as the Dog-Faced goddess, who was perpetually at war with Kefa in the struggle over the Evolutionary process. Shu was the Setting Sun, and in a certain metaphysical way he became the symbol of the declining of all activity, and thus the Lord of Gore, in the sense of being the occasion for the devouring activities of Matet being able to act upon the Forms nourished by Kefa. The next conception that grew up was that of Light and Shade as the two poles of all being, the one representing the Active and the other the Passive aspect of Nature. Shui was the name of Light and Shade. Out of this grew the conception of the Two Truths of Water and Breath, that is, the Static and Dynamic states of matter. This Dynamic Activity as the act of Breathing, or the breathing motion of the Universal Principle, was called Ssu. Then there was the conception of Kafi-Shu, that is, the Breath proceeding from Kaf or the Generatrix, hence the Generative Process engenders the Breath or the Dynamic Activity. The symbol of this was the Ape. Moi was the Mouth of Shu, that is, the channel of activity growing out of the Breathing of the Generatrix. Again Ru and Peh were the names of the symbolic mouth—feminine, or, in other words the Vulva, indicating that the speaking the word, or the breathing forth was simply another name for the giving birth to that which was breathed out. In a word, Breathing was giving birth.

They had also mastered the Law of Periodicity, and recognized that to go to the extreme in any direction was to be turned back in the opposite direction, and to this characteristic of all activity they gave the name of Khesf, and it was worshipped as a god. Also there was the extreme of possible action in any given direction, and this was called Keb, the corner, the turning point; also the four corners or the four points of returning were deified as Keb. Khut was the place of the Solar resurrection in the sense that every day was supposed to mark a new birth of the Sun, and so in this sense Anhar, the Rising Sun, was the Solar Resurrection. From this it will be seen that the religion of the pre-Mayan Egyptians was a system of Nature Worship in the strictest sense of the term. They saw nothing above the process of physical causation and evolution, and while they had learned a great deal about things, nevertheless, they held to what might be termed Physical Religion. It was, in fact, Physics Personified. And also it was viewed from a Feministic standpoint.

Into this Egyptian Religion was introduced that of the Mayan invaders. The latter adopted the forms of the original Cultus, but Apotheosised them in such a way as to form a highly Metaphysical Cultus, using the gross forms of the original Cultus as the symbols of the higher one. Out of the original crudities of the Dual Conception of the former people was evolved the Metaphysical conception of the Doctrine of the Two Truths. Among the original Egyptians this was merely a Physical Principle, but the more philosophical Mayas developed it to the point where it related to the Higher Principles of the Universe. The Two Truths became the Static and the Dynamic Principles in the Formative Sphere of the Universal Substratum. Not only were they applied to the Static and the Dynamic Poles, but also to the entire field of Duality growing out of the two opposing tendencies, and to this Duality of Causation was given the name of Ma (a Maya word meaning yes and no), hence Ma became the goddess of the Dual Truth, or the Great Paradox, and hence goddess of the Two Truths in all their ramifications. Again, there was developed the conception of Ma-Shu, the Pool of the Two Truths. Shu, remember, is Breath or the goddess of Breath, and hence Ma-Shu is the Dual Breath, that is, the outbreathing manifesting in Duality and Opposition. This Duality of Action, which is also the Duality of birth giving, engenders a Duality of Substance, or the Dual Waters, which therefore present Duality of Formation, hence we have the Waters or the Pool of the Two Truths, which is the Matrix of the Dual Formation that is to result from the Dual Breath. Shui was the god, or rather the goddess in the original form, of Breath in the sense of the Breath of the Mouth of Hathor. Now it must be borne in mind that in the Mystical sense, the Mouth is the Mons Veneris, hence Breath from the Mouth is giving birth, hence the breathing from the Mouth of Hathor means the Generatrix giving birth to that which comes forth. Hathor is therefore the Generative Potency of the Pool of Two Truths, or Ma-Ma, or the Dual Truth governing the generation of all things. From this also Hathor became the Suckler who nourishes that which has been engendered within the Pool of the Two Truths, for the Truth of Water is also the Truth of Blood, that is, the Mother Blood which nourishes the Foetus, and which later specializes the Lacteal Fluid which the child lives upon. This nutritive principle in the Pool of the Two Truths therefore becomes the Nursing Mother in the Mystical Sense, and hence Hathor is made the Suckler or the Wet Nurse of the Gods, in the sense of the Dual Truth acting as the Nourisher of all those Specialized States that emanate from this Principle of Duality. Her Totem was therefore the Cow. Ab-Khu was the variegated plumes, the variegated plumes being the two Ostrich Plumes, one representing Light and the other Shade, which, when given to Ma, indicated that the source of the differentiation of Light and Shade was in the Duality of Truth. Shu-Ma was the Image of the Great Waters, that is to say, the Dual Breath was the Activity of the Pool of the Two Truths. Shu, the Double Breath, is also the same as the Goddess AA-ur, the Very Great, or in other words, it is this activity of the Dual Truth that engenders the Kosmic Pleroma. From this it will be seen that the Cultus of Ma was merely the elevation of the older Cultus of Kaf, Kefa and Shu from the Physical to the highest plane of Formation and to the realm of the Logos and the Formative Mind.

Growing out of this conception of the Dual Truth in all of its manifestations was the conception of a Formative Principle of Generation which we might term the Waters of Formation; this was called Typhon or Seti, and in the original form of the conception was feminine. This was the Typhonian Generatrix of the Waters, and was identical with the Moist Nature of Hermes, and was also the same as the Mayan Xmucane, or Female Vigor. Out of this Typhonian Water of Formation was generated Sesennu, the agitating, distracting, tormenting and fighting principle, or the Active Breath of the Waters of Formation, which was male, and, being the engendered result of the Typhonian Waters, it was the son of those Waters. This son, or Energy, soon dominated the movements of the Waters of Formation, and hence became the husband of his mother. In this way was born Set-Typhon, or the male Typhon. He was the same as Xpukakok or the Masculine Principle, the Father of the gods. In the course of time this Masculine Principle became Osiris and the Feminine Principle Isis. Kaf, or the Old Generatrix, became the Great Harlot, because she had no husband or directive energy to control her, and the same term was applied to the state of the Waters, of the Celestial Waters of Formation, for now the Universal Causation was viewed as being through the double sexed arrangement, with the Masculine Principle in control, and this was the actual state of Evolution at this stage of the Universe.

Quetzalcoatl, or the Universe as the ever changing sequence growing out of the Formative Action of the Great Mother, became Ra. And here we have the explanation of the apparent contradiction in the Egyptian Kosmogony, for, in the true Kosmical sense of the word, Ra was the son of Isis and Osiris the same as was Quetzalcoatl the son of Xmucane and Xpukakok, but in spite of this he is ever represented as ruling the Universe before the Reign of Osiris. The meaning is this, Ra is the Universe as the ever-changing sequence growing out of the Formative Waters.

of the Upper Heaven, under whatsoever name they
may appear. As such, He was first engendered by
Typhon, the husbandless Generatrix of the heavenly
realm of formation, and continued from that time on
without a break. In the course of time there was a
change in the Waters of Formation as well as the
change in the conception of that principle, hence that
which had been the Typhonian Generatrix became
Isis, and as She from that time forth was the Generatrix of Ra, He was supposed to be Her son, that is,
in the Evolutionary sense, and yet Ra was older than
Isis. While Isis was the Consort of Osiris, she was
nevertheless the Virgin of the World, the meaning of
this being that She was the continuity of that Formative Process that had in times past been without a
husband. That is to say, She was not another Principle of Formation, but rather a new evolution of the
original Waters of Formation. Sesennu is also the
Place of the Eight. The Seven are the Seven Fires
of Gestation of the Great Mother, no matter under
what form she is presented, and the Eighth is of necessity that which gives rise to the seven. In other words,
it is the Masculine Fecundating Activity that causes
the Feminine Gestative Potency, therefore that Masculine Activity which was Set-Typhon and later became
Osiris was the Eighth, ruling the Seven Rulers of
Hermes, who were identical with the Gucumatz.

The Heart of Heaven was divided into three conceptions, and for each there was a god. The Heart
That Thinks, or Primordial Ideation, became Kneph,
or the Divine Serpent, Male-Female, also called Amun,
and likewise Amen-Ra, because Ra or the Universe
as the ever changing sequence of Evolution is in last
analysis the manifestation of Primordial Ideation.
This Amen-Ra or Kneph is also the All-Father Mind
of Hermes. The Mouth That Speaks the Thoughts
of the Heart, or the Creative Potency of Primordial
Ideation as the Divine Fiat was Ptah, who was represented as being hatched from an egg held in the mouth
of the Divine Serpent, Kneph, that is to say, Ptah is
the Word or uttered thought of Kneph or Primordial
Ideation. The Eyes That See, or the Directive Activity of the Fiat, the manifestation of the Fiat, which
directs the Evolution of the Universe, was termed

Taht, or Kosmic Thought. This Taht, or Kosmic Thought, is Dual in its nature, consisting of the Logos or Reason, which is at all times at-oned with Primordial Ideation and the Creative Word, which is the Masculine Aspect, and also of the Formative Mind, which directs the Formative Action of the Celestial Waters, or Isis. This latter aspect of Kosmic Thought was the Syzygy of the Logos and was Seket, the same as Ma in one of her aspects, though Ma at all times represents the Duality of Truth, while this Syzygy of Taht is simply the Mind governing the Formative Activity of the Waters of Space. Also it is to be borne in mind that Taht was originally the Moon God, but by the Mayas he was made the Directive Thought of the Kosmos.

After the new order of things was introduced, and the Formative Principle had evolved into Isis and Osiris and they had brought forth Ra again so that the Universal Sequence was in accordance with the New Arrangement, the Earth itself, that is, the Earth Spirit, was reborn, in the sense that it conformed to that Order of Evolution, and that is what is meant by the birth of Horus, for Horus is the same as Votan, or the Earth Spirit after it has been transformed in accordance with the Isis-Osiris Formation. The myth of the war between Typhon and Horus in reality relates to the great struggle in the Earth between the old Typhonian and the later Isis-Osiris mode of Creative Activity. It was the struggle in the earth as to whether the Feminine or the Masculine-Feminine Principle of Formation was to control it. The Reign of Horus was the period during which the Earth was perfectly expressing the New Phase of Evolution. The reign of Osiris was the period during which the Masculine Principle of Formation ruled in the Formative Sphere. This was at last overcome by the Typhonian principle and the result was the reign of Isis, during which the New Great Mother was the sole power in the Formative Sphere. At last we have the time when Horus tore the crown from her head and ruled the country, and the meaning is that when the Osiris power was perfectly expressed through the earth the Feminine Formative Principle was deprived of its power, and the Earth entered upon a period of Mascu-

line dominance, during which the Feminine Principle
has been subjected to its Syzygy all the time.

We have therefore a period of readjustment which
lasted for a considerable length of time, during which
the original Egyptian Cultus of the Great Mother was
being absorbed by the Mayan Conception, and the
ultimate merging of the two so that they became
largely the same system. However, it is to be borne
in mind that for a long time there was the original
Cultus of the earlier people, and they could not understand the more abstract views of the Mayas, and it was
necessary to make them believe that the two religions
were the same. This was accomplished by reason of
the fact that the Mayas were all members of the Hermetic Brotherhood. They formed the Egyptian Section of the Brotherhood, which kept the true teaching from the Multitude and taught the Mysteries as
they really were to the Elect. To the Multitude they
were Priests of the Old Gods to a great extent, and
showed them that the gods they worshiped were the
same as the ancient gods, but what they did not do
was to show the Metaphysical aspect of the matter.
In a word they inculcated the ancient Nature Worship
among the People, though eliminating the Feminine
Conception as it had been in the former times, and
tending to purify it to some extent all the way through.
For the more advanced they formed what they called
the Order of Ra, which was simply the two lower
Degrees of the Hermetic Brotherhood and in this they
inculcated those Principles which were to prepare one
for the mysteries contained in the Higher Degrees.
But for a long time none but Mayas were permitted
to enter the Higher Degrees of the Brotherhood, the
Hermetic Degrees. In the course of time, when the
two Races had been completely merged into the Historical Egyptians, they continued this exclusiveness
as to admitting any of the Lower Classes into the Mysteries. This is the real cause of the exclusiveness of
the Egyptian Brotherhood to the present day. In harmony with all the other Hermetic and Mayan nations
the Egyptians continued to make the King the Hierarchal Head of the Order, or the Brotherhood, until
in the course of several thousand years the Kings lost
their Spirituality and their knowledge so that they

were no longer fitted to occupy the position. From
that time forth they were still the head of the outer
religion, but the Hermetic Brotherhood operated in
Secret and had its own Elder Brothers, initiating the
King into as much of the mysteries as he could bear.

## THE PERSIAN BROTHERHOOD.

The Persian Nagas being Mayas, were of necessity connected with the Maya Brotherhood, and hence were Hermetic. However, there were very few of them connected with the Higher Hermetic Degrees. The first development of the cultus was that of Mithras, who was identical with Quetzalcoatl, but who in later times was connected more with the Sun than with the Feathered Serpent. However, we see this Quetzalcoatl worship under both heads, for this was the basis of the Ophiolatry of the Persian Nagas. But above everything else, Mithras was the Sun, or rather the Man of the Sun, that is, the Universe, as the Sequence of Creative Evolution, the same as Quetzalcoatl. It was to a great extent to Mithras that human sacrifices were offered.

The Guchumatz were viewed as the Seven Fires, and hence Fire was worshipped in their honor. The Persian Fire Cultus was the Cultus of the Seven Fires, or the Guchumatz. They were also worshipped under the form of Serpents.

The Persians also had their Magi, the same as the Chaldeans, and as the Magi were the priesthood of the Anthropos, or the Archetypal Man (see articles on the Akkadians, Chaldeans and the Shepherd of Men in Temple Talks), it follows that they were originally devoted to a Cultus of the Archetypal Man or the Anthropos.

In the course of time, the Degree connected with the Mystery of the Heart of Heaven was developed into a Cultus that overshadows all of the other Cults. Out of the Unmanifest Essence, Zarvan Akarana (endless, limitless duration, or time without limit), there was supposed to emanate two Principles, Ahura

Mazda, the Good Principle, and Arhiman, the Evil
Principle. At the same time it is well to bear in mind
that Ahura Mazda is Light, while Arhiman is Darkness, hence they are Light and Shade, the same as
the First Aspect of the Doctrine of the Two Truths,
and Ma, goddess of the Two Truths of the Egyptians.
Now, as Ma is a Mayan term meaning Yes and No,
and as Ma as a goddess is the goddess of the Dual
Truth, it follows that Ahura Mazda and Arhiman are
in the first place the gods of Duality. To the Initiates
they were known to be identical, and merely the two
poles of the same principle, as the Duality of all Manifestation; but to the profane, they were two distinct
divine beings, forever at war with each other. After
the Iranian period the latter were never.initiated into
the Mystery, and out of the mystery of the Duality
of Truth there grew up the belief in Good and Evil
as Eternal Verities with a Good and a Bad Principle.
Out of this has grown the Satan superstition, but Dia-
bolos est Deus inversus. In the first development of
the Cultus of Ahura Mazda and Arhiman we have the
Cultus of the Two Truths, but Ahura Mazda did not
stop there. He was also Good Thought. In this sense
He became the Heart of Heaven, at least in its lowest aspect. In other words, He was Kosmic Thought
or Taht. However, we see in later developments of
the Cultus the idea of a Reflection of Ahura Mazda.
His shadow as it were cast into Kosmos, which is
sometimes called his Good Thought, so that Ahura
Mazda is not so much Good Thought as the Good
Thinker, who manifests as Good Thought. In this
sense his Good Thought is Kosmic Thought, or the
Eyes that See, while Ahura Mazda is Phta or the
Mouth that Speaks, the Second Person in the Mayan
Trinity.

There was never any definite Cultus of the Heart
that Thinks, though the place was undoubtedly as-
signed to the Unmanifest, or Time without Limit.

The other Cultus, and the most beautiful of all, was
that of Ainyahita, who was to the profane the Moon
Goddess, but to the Initiates the same as Xmucane,
that is, the Great Mother. She was in the Mysteries
the Mother of Mithras, and the Daughter of Ahura
Mazda, though in some of the popular Cults she was

the wife of Mithras, but in the Mysteries she had no husband, but was the Feminine Genatrix without a husband, and hence very similar to Kaf among the Egyptians. She was, however, the perpetual Virgin and the Virgin of the World. It was from her that the Virgin Mother Cultus of the Persians was derived, though this was a very Sacred Mystery, not to be profaned. The mythus of Ainyahita relates to the introduction of a cycle of change in the process of Kosmical Evolution, in which she is the means of regenerating the Universe, through the rebirth of Mithras, and also through her subjugation to Ahura Mazda. It is impossible to get at the true meaning through either the Avesta or the fragments for the reason that they are not frank, and cover up the meaning entirely. The mystery, however, will be understood when we bear in mind that Ainyahita is the Great Mother Principle and at the same time the Virgin of the World, who is perpetually gestating the Universe or Mithras and also bringing him forth, hence it is to be borne in mind that he is not something born, but rather a sequence in perpetual process of being born. Ainyahita is represented as a Virgin who is loving the Universe into the proper shape. At the same time her devotion to Ahura Mazda causes her to be the modulating chord, so to speak, through which the Thought of Ahura Mazda molds the Universe continually.

Her covenant shows what she is: "I am upon the Earth to reclaim the Earth, to make of the Desert a Paradise, a Paradise most suitable unto God (Ahura Mazda) and His Associates to dwell therein." This indicates that the transformation of the Universe is her mission, and that is a work that can only be accomplished by the gestative power of the Great Mother, and as she is the Perpetual Virgin she is therefore the Virgin Mother or Virgin of the World, the same as Isis, though without a husband. See the Fragments of Ainyahita, translated by Dr. H'anish, for the full story. There was a farther development of the Persian Mysteries in the Cultus of Zarathustra, but as that is so well known, it is scarcely worth while to discuss it, as it was but a development of the Mazda Cultus.

## THE HERMETIC BROTHERHOOD OF ELEPHANTIS

The Nagas who settled in India and the adjacent countries being all of them members of the Maya Brotherhood in some Degree of Initiation, soon founded a Section of the Brotherhood in their new home. The great center of this Brotherhood was in Elephantis, and hence it soon became known as the Hermetic Brotherhood of Elephantis; but this name was not confined to the Temples at that place, but was applied to the entire Brotherhood among all of the Southern Nagas. Because of the different Degrees of Initiation and the fact that each Degree became in a sense a separate Cultus, there was a great divergence in the Religion of the Indian Nagas.

We must guard against the mistake of confusing the popular Religion of the Nagas with the Esoteric teaching of the Brotherhood. The most popular of all the Cults was that of the Nagas, or Gucumatz. This was represented by the Seven-Headed Serpent, and also by the Seven Snakes. In this Cultus the Rattlesnake of their ancestors became the Cobra of India, and the Cobra was worshiped as the Sacred Ophis symbol. This was also worshiped as the Seven Fires, and from that aspect as the Seven Lights. The Altar of the Seven-Headed Serpent was at all times furnished with the Seven Lights. It was to this Sevenfold Serpent that human sacrifices were in the course of time offered in the popular Cultus. However, the real Initiates knew at all times that this was not the true worship, but they did not interfere with the only means that would teach the people the true meaning of the Seven Nagas or the Seven Fires or the Seven Lights, for only by human sacrifice is it possible to impress upon the vulgar the mystery of Life and Death as One.

Another of the popular Cults was that of the Great Serpent, or the Sun, which was the same as Quetzalcoatl. He was worshiped in the Ancient Form with offerings of fruits and flowers. In the Solar Mysteries, which were the same as the Mysteries of the Great Serpent, the true nature of the Universe as the

Sequence of Creative Evolution was revealed, but this was not given to the profane, so they were permitted to worship Him instead of understanding the Mystery. He was among those who had some degree of understanding of the Mystery the most beloved of all the gods, for his Mysteries were those of Redemption through the Vicarious Sacrifice of the Universe. Purusha sacrificing Himself for the Race is the survival of that Cultus. He is the Crucified Savior of all the Religions of the earth. However, it is not the Crucifixion of a man, but the Crucifixion of the Universe upon the Cross of Life, that is to say, the continual death of the Universe, that through such death it may be born again, hence He dies for Himself but this Self Redemption through Evolution is the means of uplifting all Life. The ancient Mass was the Celebration of this Redemption of the Universe through its own Death.

There was also the Cultus of the Great Mother, or Xmucane, which became that of Maha-Devi. This was identical with the Great Mother Cultus everywhere, that is, it was the Revelation of the Mystery of the Formative Principle of Nature, that which was manifested through the Harmony of the Seven Serpents. In the Popular Cultus there grew up a conception of her very similar to that of the Ishtar Cultus of the Akkadians. She was conceived not only as the Great Mother, but also as the Great Harlot, because all Formation was developed within her, and thus she was perpetually giving birth, hence she must be in a continual state of copulation. To the Initiates it was understood that she was Dual and in this sense was the Genatrix within herself in the same way as in the Egyptian Cultus, and that it was perfectly Kosmical; but to the multitude this was not known, so they developed a Cultus in which sexual impurity was the dominant element of her worship. As a result of this, there were kept Temple Virgins, as they were called, who were in fact not Virgins at all, though they were not married. These girls were the Priestesses or Sacred Courtesans of Maha-Devi and the nautch girls of the modern Hindoo Cultus are the survivals of this practice. At the time that this was practiced there was a secret Cultus in which her nature as the Virgin Mother was taught, and here the most austere purity was enjoined. The devotees of the Virgin Mother were required to lead a life of the most austere self-discipline and to mortify the flesh. She was supposed to have no mercy on anyone who was dominated by carnal desire, and therefore they had to mortify the flesh until all lust was dead. She was the Mother, but the Mother who did not believe in sparing the rod! Also it was recognized that Her great effort was to bring forth children upon Her own Plane, that is, within the Formative Sphere, above the Harmony of the Seven Fires. To do this it was essential that all of the Energies of the Seven Serpents, and of the Nature devoid of Reason that sprang from the activity of those Energies should become de-energized within the soul. Thus it was that before she could give birth to one in this Region of the Eighth she must de-energize all of the Seven Energies, and this would amount to the destruction of all their soul below this Formative Sphere. In this way she had to destroy them on all the Lower Planes of Action before she could bear them on her own Plane. In this way she became the Destructress as well as the Genatrix. Thus she was the Mother and at the same time the very embodiment of Wanton Destruction. In this aspect we see her still preserved in the Hindoo Kali, which is a Spiritual Apotheosis of Durga, who was the Virgin Mother as the Destructress. As a result of this conception, human sacrifice was naturally offered to her, and in later times, to a great extent, animal sacrifice. Then she was the one who required the sacrifice of Human Life to her, so that she might in this way draw her children to her bosom. In this sense she became Bhovanee, who is worshiped to this day among the Javanese descendants of the Nagas. The Bhovanee Cultus, which gave rise to the Thugs, is a pure Naga Cultus. She is represented with the sweetest face conceivable, for she is the mother anxious to clasp her children to her bosom, and this she does through their death. This led in the course of time to a regular Cult of murder, that is, the killing of people so that they might go to the bosom of Bhovanee. Of course this was a perversion of the true Cultus, for the death which Bhovanee demanded was a purely mystical one, and her children who were clasped to her bosom were still living in the Physical

Body. This shows the great danger which is at all
times attendant upon the giving of the Sacred Mysteries in any form to the Vulgar. They are sure to
materialize them, and give to them a physical form.
It is in this way that anything so sacred as the Mystery of the Virgin Mother-Destructress became the
cause of human sacrifice and ritual murder, and that
the Cultus of the Great Harlot became the cause of
ritualistic inchastity. Such Divine Mysteries should
not be mentioned to the Profane at all. She was worshiped as the Cow-goddess, as the Bearer and the
Suckler, which connects her with Hathor and Kefa
in the Egyptian Cultus.

The Cultus that was held by the most Spiritual of
all the Initiates was that of the Heart of Heaven. This
had the same meaning to them that it had to the
Mayas and all the other Initiates of the mystic Fourth
Degree. That is to say, it was Primordial Ideation,
the Activity of that Ideation, manifesting as Primordial Will, in the form of the Formative Aspect of the
Ultimate Spirit, in a word the Formative Potency of
Primordial Mind, and lastly the Kosmic Manifestation of that Primordial Ideation in the form of Kosmic Ideation or Taht. There were not so many thousands in the Old Days who were ever Initiated into
this Mystery, for it was reserved for the most holy
of the people, and for them alone. The Heart of
Heaven was with them, in common with all the other
Mayan races, a Double-Sexed Divinity, and hence
there was not in this Cultus any element of sex worship. It was this element that kept it in perfect purity
during all the time of the Naga period. The Heart
of Heaven was conceived in two aspects, or we might
say in three. There was first of all the Heart that
Thinks and the Mouth that Speaks, or Primordial
Ideation and the Formative Trend of this Ideation,
which was identical with the Primordial Will, and its
aspect of Neucleation. To this was given the name
of Bodhi. There was also conceived the Action of
this Bodhi in Nature, so that there was manifested
the Kosmic Thought or Kosmic Reason, as the Mirroring of Primordial Ideation in Nature, as the Logos
or Taht; to this was given the name of Buddh or
Reason; also the Formative Mind, as the Norm of
Synthesis, which acts upon the Formative Sphere or

Region of the Eighth, Maha-Devi. Because this was the Formative Intelligence, determining all the Synthetic Operations of the Kosmos, and hence the Norm of Integration, they gave to it the name Dharma, meaning originally the Trunk of a Tree, in the sense of being the source of all the Accretive Operation of the Formative Principle. It was also conceived as that which binds together and unites as a perfect Synthesis. It was, in fact, the Intelligence directing the Formative Principle of Maha-Devi. Quite often, however, they confused the two aspects of the Kosmic Reason under the common name of Buddh, Reason. This was the same as the Eyes that See, the Third Person in the Trinity. This was quite natural, as the Heart of Heaven was Dual-Sexed, and the Logos is Masculine and the Formative Mind the Feminine Counterpart or Syzygy of the Logos. Those who were initiates of this Mystery of the Heart of Heaven, of the Mystic Fourth Degree, became in the course of time known as Buddhists, as Initiates into the Mystery of the Buddh or Kosmic Reason. They were the same as the Past Epopts in the other Sections of the Brotherhood. When they were made perfect in this Mystery, and had become Initiates into the higher Mystery of Bodhi they were called Arahats.

In the course of time there appeared another conception, such as had never been fully developed in any of the other Sections of the Brotherhood. That was the conception of the periodical incarnation of the Buddh in the soul of some one man. This person might be a great Hierophant, or he might be one of less degree, though he was invariably one of royal blood. When the incarnation took place, he became the Supreme Head of the Hierarchy, no matter what his previous position had been. This was most natural, for the Fourth Degree was the last Degree of the Brotherhood, and it was only natural that the Incarnation of the Buddh should be the hierarchal head of the students of that Mystery. There were a great many of these incarnations, called Buddhas, or Fully Enlightened Ones, that is, ones in which the full light of the Buddh was Incarnate, during the 10,000 years from the settlement of India to the invasion of the Aryan Barbarians. However, all of the Buddhas were not Nagas, for they recognized among the Hierophants of the Fourth Degree in other Sections of the Brotherhood many of the same degree of attainment, and to these they also gave the title of Buddha. However, at long intervals of time there appeared a man in whom not only the Buddh but even the Supreme Bodhi or Primordial Ideation was fully incarnate, and to such they gave the title of Buddhas Great, or Supreme Buddhas, that is, incarnations of both Buddh and Bodhi. All together there were only three of these Great Buddhas during the 10,000 years of the Naga Period. The Buddhists or Initiates into the Mystery of the Buddh, and particularly the Mystery of Bodhi, the Heart that Thinks, were fully conversant with the mystical meaning of all the lower Degrees, and hence they knew that the gods were merely states of the universal Operations through Creative Evolution. Therefore they worshiped nothing, but understood the meaning of all things, both in the Uncreate and in the realm of Creation. Knowing all of those things they were above the Illusion cast by them, and formed for themselves a Law that was derived directly from the source of all Truth in the Bosom of the Heart that Thinks, or Bodhi.

Knowing the source of the entire evolutionary process to be in the Primordial Ideation of Bodhi or the Heart that Thinks, they realized that the natural processes were but the mirroring in Nature of the Pure Ideation of the Heart of Heaven. Knowing the Ultimate Cause of all things, they were Masters of the Law of Causation in its ultimate bearings. This knowledge they called the Doctrine of the Heart, that is, the Doctrine or Law which was revealed by the Ideation of the Heart of Heaven, and which they contrasted to the Doctrine of the Eye, or the knowledge which one had to derive from a study of the Evolutionary process in operation in Nature. Thus the Doctrine of the Eye was derived from the study of the evolutionary process itself, while the Doctrine of the Heart was the result of the direct Intuition of the Eternal Norms governing and being mirrored in that evolutionary process. This Doctrine of the Heart, which was proclaimed afresh by every Great Buddha, and for the proclamation of which He appeared whenever it was entirely lost sight of, was the final consummation of all the Naga Mysteries. The mere understanding of this doctrine was supposed to bring one into the realization of the highest Goal or Nirvana. This remained the supreme Cultus of India until the invasion of the Arvan Barbarians brought the Mysteries to an end.

Printed in July 2021
by Rotomail Italia S.p.A., Vignate (MI) - Italy